505 WINE QUESTIONS

YOUR FRIENDS CAN'T ANSWER

The 505 Series:

505 Baseball Questions Your Friends Can't Answer—Kingston
505 Football Questions Your Friends Can't Answer—Rosenthal
505 Hockey Questions Your Friends Can't Answer—Polnaszek
505 Basketball Questions Your Friends Can't Answer—Barzman
505 Boxing Questions Your Friends Can't Answer—Sugar & Grasso

505 Rock 'n' Roll Questions Your Friends Can't Answer—Schaffner & Schaffner
505 Theatre Questions Your Friends Can't Answer—Beaufort
505 Movie Questions Your Friends Can't Answer—Phillips
505 Television Questions Your Friends Can't Answer—Castleman & Podrazik

Also by Carole Collier

The Natural Sugarless Dessert Cookbook (Walker)
Woman's Day Gelatin Cookery
Woman's Day Serving Food With Style
Rodale's Soups And Salads
Feasting On Raw Foods

505 WINE QUESTIONS
YOUR FRIENDS CAN'T ANSWER

CAROLE COLLIER

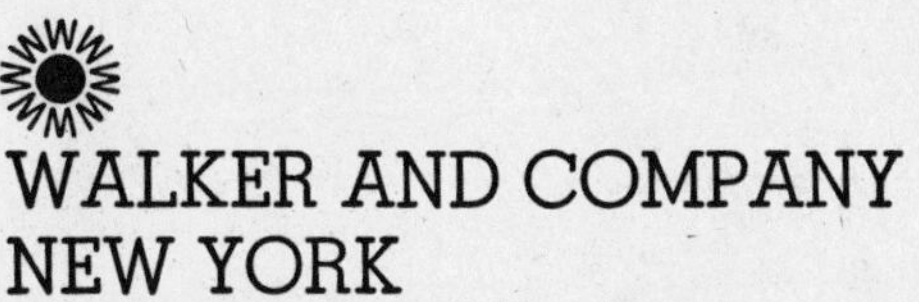

WALKER AND COMPANY
NEW YORK

This book is dedicated to
Ken Maguire

For cellar raids that made me smile
For San Francisco, Carmel, and the vineyards of California,
For New York State, Pennsylvania, Portugal and Spain,
For sharing every pleasure and never complaining,
Thank you.

First published in the United States of America in 1983 by the Walker Publishing Company, Inc.

Published simultaneously in Canada by John Wiley & Sons Canada, Limited, Rexdale, Ontario.

ISBN: 0-8027-0730-0 (cloth)
0-8027-7209-9 (paperback)

Library of Congress Catalog Card Number: 82-40440

Printed in the United States of America

10 9 8 7 6 5 4 3 2 1

Library of Congress Cataloging in Publication Data
Collier, Carole
1. Wine and wine making—Miscellanea. I. Title.
II. Title: Five hundred five wine questions your friends can't answer.
TP548.C64 1983 641.2'22 82-40440
ISBN 0-8027-0730-3
ISBN 0-8027-7209-9 (pbk.)

CONTENTS

INTRODUCTION

It's a curious thing about wine; the more you learn about it, the less you realize you know. On the other hand, the more you learn, the more you are able to appreciate and enjoy the wine you drink.

Acquiring knowledge and sharing it with others is a passion among wine lovers, second only to experiencing vinous flavors on the palate. And those who truly enjoy wine equally delight in discussing the subject, no matter how limited or copious their knowledge.

In selecting the 505 wine questions for this book, an effort was made to include material for three levels of enophiles: those who are just beginning to develop an interest; those who are relatively expert; and those whom Reginald* might rank as authentic wine snobs.

Rather than deliberately trying to outwit your friends with tricky word play, I have attempted to compose questions (and answers) that might be considered as interesting and entertaining as they are enlightening. A certain amount of so-called trivia has been incorporated, along with much practical knowledge useful to wine appreciation, specifically for that reason.

In any event, it is hoped that the 505 wine questions will impart something of the fascination of wine to your friends—and you—and shed some light on its many mysteries.

*The main character in Leonard S. Bernstein's *The Official Guide to Wine Snobbery.*

FLIGHT I

Viniculture— Winemaking

Viticulture— Grape Growing

Viniculture—Winemaking

Wine is light held together by water.
Galileo

1. What is wine?
   a) the naturally fermented juice of fresh ripe grapes
   b) the distilled juice of fresh ripe grapes
   c) the naturally fermented juice of any fresh ripe fruit
   d) the distilled juice of any fresh ripe fruit

2. What term is used for the juice of grapes before it is fermented into wine?
   a) pomace
   b) must
   c) cuvée
   d) brix

3. What is free-run juice?

4. Where does the tannin in wine come from?
   a) the skins of the grapes
   b) the seeds of the grapes
   c) the stems of the grapes
   d) the wood in oak barrels
   e) all of the above

5. Can white wine be made from red grapes?

6. Yeast and sugar are the principal ingredients of fermentation. What are the principal by-products?

a) alcohol
b) carbon monoxide
c) carbon dioxide
d) sulfur dioxide

7. During fermentation, the grape sugar in the must is converted to:
a) alcohol
b) carbon dioxide
c) wine

8. If the fermentation temperature is kept very low, the resulting wine will be:
a) low in acid and alcohol
b) darker in color
c) tart and acidic
d) fresh and fruity

9. Malolactic fermentation is a secondary fermentation that is caused by the presence of lactic acid bacteria in some wines. What effect or effects does malolactic fermentation have on wine?
a) The malic acid (one of the major organic acids in grapes) is converted to lactic acid and carbon dioxide.
b) It lowers the fixed acidity in wine.
c) It enhances the flavor complexity of the wine.
d) It stabilizes the wine by assuring that a secondary fermentation will not take place after the wine is bottled.

10. What is the process of carefully drawing off the wine from its lees by siphoning or pumping called?
a) fining
b) racking
c) filtering
d) centrifuging

11. What is the method of clearing the wine of suspended particles by the addition of substances such as egg whites, casein, or bentonite called?

a) fining
b) filtering
c) centrifuging
d) ion exchange

12. What result or results does barrel aging accomplish?
a) It imparts wood extract to the wine.
b) It oxidizes the wine.
c) It reduces the fruitiness of the wine.
d) It increases the complexity of the wine.

13. Can you number the following winemaking steps in their correct order?
a) fermenting on the skins
b) filtering
c) harvesting
d) pressing
e) crushing
f) aging
g) racking
h) fining

14. Officially, what is the maximum alcoholic content of table wines?
a) 12%
b) 14%
c) 16%
d) 18%

15. This man succeeded in identifying the microorganisms that make grape juice ferment, and he established the role of oxygen in the maturing of wine and the way in which it affects color. Who is he?

16. Who is the Russian-born, French-trained microbiologist who came to America in 1938 and has since influenced the style of California wines more than anyone else?

ANSWERS

1. *a. By official designation, wine is the pure, naturally fermented juice of fresh ripe grapes. If wine is made from other fruit, the fruit must be indicated on the label, followed by the word wine; for example, apple wine or plum wine.*

2. *b. It is called must up to the point when fermentation is complete, at which time the product becomes wine. Pomace is the fermented pulp or solids left behind after the wine has been drawn off. Cuvée refers to a blend of still wines, and brix is the term used when measuring the sugar content of must or wine.*

3. *The term* free-run *refers to the juice that flows freely from the grapes after they are crushed, but before they are pressed.*

4. e. *Tannin, a phenolic compound, is naturally present in the roots, wood, stems, skins and seeds of many plants, including grapevines. It is present in varying degrees in practically all wines, and because it acts as an antioxidant, it contributes to the longevity of wines.*

Tannin may be noticed as a dry, harsh feeling on the tongue and teeth and also as a bitterness at the back of the throat, especially in young red wines. As wines age, tannin forms part of the normal sediment that drops to the bottom of the bottle, so that a mature wine has less tannin than a young wine.

Because red wines are fermented with the skins, seeds, and sometimes the stems of the grapes, tannin may be present to a great degree. In white and rosé wines the amount is hardly noticeable, although some tannin is extracted from the minimal skin contact and/or through pressing. Barrel aging may also impart tannin from the oak of the container.

5. *Yes. With few exceptions, wine grapes, both red and white, have clear, colorless juice. The coloring elements (pigments) that* *make a wine red, rosé, or white are contained in the skins of the grapes. The amount of time that the juice and the skins are allowed to remain in contact with each other when the grapes are crushed and fermented determines the color intensity of the finished wine. Thus, white wine can be and is made from red grapes by immediately separating the juice from the skins when the grapes are crushed.*

6. *a, c. Alcohol and carbon dioxide are the principal by-products of fermentation. When making still (non-sparkling) table wines, the carbon dioxide is allowed to dissipate.*

7. *a. The grape sugar is converted to alcohol through the action of the yeasts. The sweeter the grapes, the higher the potential alcohol level, assuming fermentation is allowed to proceed to its natural conclusion.*

8. *d. A cool temperature allows for a longer, but gentler fermentation, which preserves more of the fruit and freshness in the grapes.*

9. *a, b, c, d.*

10. *b. racking.*

11. *a. fining.*

12. *a, b, c, d.*

13. *1–c, 2–e, 3–a, 4–d, 5–g, 6–f, 7–h, 8–b.*

14. *b. 14%. However, federal law permits a leeway of 1.5% in either direction of the amount specified on the label. Thus, a wine that lists 14% alcohol on its label may in fact contain anywhere between 12.5 and 15.5% alcohol.*

15. *Louis Pasteur (1822–1895).*

16. *André Tchelistcheff, who is also known as "the winemakers' winemaker."*

Viticulture—Grape Growing

. . . the wine must taste of its own grape.
Elizabeth Barrett Browning

1. In botanical classification, all of the world's grapevines belong to a single genus. What is it called?

2. Within the genus mentioned above, there are many species of vines, of which only a few are of value to the winemaker. *Vitis vinifera* is an example of a species that was:
a) brought to North America from Europe by early settlers
b) found growing wild in America when the white man arrived
c) created by man through a genetic crossing of two other species

3. *Vitis labrusca* is an example of a useful species that was (a, b, or c, in Question 2)?

4. Of the two species *labrusca* and *vinifera,* which produces the finest wines?

5. What is the process of splicing a grapevine to North American rootstock called?
a) hybridizing
b) genetic crossing
c) grafting

6. What is the name of the root parasite, indigenous to the eastern United States, that was accidentally brought to Europe, where it spread and devastated the vineyards of most winemaking countries in the late 1800s?

7. What is the term for the crossing of different species, varieties, strains, or clones to create new or different grape varieties that combine the best qualities of both parents?
   a) enology
   b) ampelography
   c) hybridization

8. Who were Albert Seibel (1844–1936), Eugene Kuhlmann (1858–1932), François Baco (1865–1947), and Pierre Landot (1900–1942)?
   a) the first men to plant *vinifera* vines in the eastern United States
   b) French hybridizers
   c) founders of the State Agricultural Experiment Station at Geneva, New York
   d) discoverers of native American grape varieties, which were subsequently named for their finders

9. Although he was not the first to import French-American hybrid varieties into the United States, he is widely credited with being the man who did the most to popularize them. Who is he?

10. An early champion (late 1940s) of hybrids and *vinifera* in Canada, this transplanted Frenchman, who worked for Bright's Wines, Ltd., had a popular hybrid variety named in his honor. What is the grape variety, and who is the man?

11. What grape varieties are the wines of eastern America made from?
    a) native American varieties
    b) hybrid varieties
    c) *vinifera* varieties

12. Indicate whether the following grapes are native American varieties (N), hybrid varieties (H), or *vinifera* varieties (V).

1. Aurora	11. Diamond
2. Baco Noir	12. Dutchess
3. Catawba	13. Emerald Riesling
4. Cayuga White	14. Foch
5. Chancellor	15. Gewürztraminer
6. Chardonnay	16. Niagara
7. Chelois	17. Ravat
8. Concord	18. White Riesling
9. De Chaunac	19. Ruby Cabernet
10. Delaware	20. Seyval Blanc

13. Which of the following wine grapes has Zinfandel in its parentage?
a) Seyval Blanc
b) Baco Noir
c) Cayuga White

14. Generally, what is the time period between the planting of a vine and its yield of grapes for winemaking?
a) two years
b) three years
c) four years
d) five years

15. Generally, the more grapes produced per acre, the finer the wine. True or false?

16. The best wines tend to come from vines grown in rich, fertile valleys. True or false?

17. If you were to plant a vineyard in order to produce fine wine, approximately how many tons of grapes would you expect each acre to yield?
a) 1–1.5 tons
b) 4–5 tons
c) 10–12 tons

18. Approximately how much wine can be produced from one acre of ripe grapes?

19. What is the meaning of the term *microclimate* (frequently used in conjunction with the location of a vineyard site)?
a) a limited area of land artificially improved by installing wind barriers, irrigation, anti-frost heaters, and other such devices
b) a general region, such as Napa Valley, where grapes have proven to grow exceedingly well
c) a limited area within a region that, because of land contour, altitude, soil type, water proximity, or other physical reasons, is more suitable to grape growing than its surrounding countryside

20. Can you match each of the following men with his best-known accomplishment?

1. John Adlum	5. Pierre Galet
2. Ephraim Wales Bull	6. Agoston Haraszthy
3. Charles Fournier	7. Jean Louis Vignes
4. Dr. Konstantin Frank	

a) proved *vinifera* vines could be grown in the eastern United States, and is known as the father of vinifera
b) one of the premier ampelography (grape description and identification) experts in the world
c) founded Buena Vista Winery in Sonoma County and laid the foundation for the California wine industry with his many accomplishments in grape growing and winemaking
d) developed the Concord grape, which skyrocketed to fame. Nevertheless, he died a poor man, and his epitaph reads, "He sowed, but others reaped."
e) Pennsylvania viticulturist who introduced and propagated the Catawba grape in the early 1800s
f) a champion of both *vinifera* and hybrids in the eastern United States; he gave Dr. Konstantin Frank a chance
g) the first to plant *vinifera* varietals in California at his El

Aliso Vineyard, on the site of Los Angeles's Union Station, in 1833

21. Following are just some of the *vinifera* varieties that are grown to produce the greatest wines of the United States. Can you match them with the European wine regions where they are most popular?

1. Cabernet Sauvignon	a) Burgundy, France
2. Chardonnay	b) Bordeaux, France
3. Merlot	c) Côtes du Rhône, France
4. Sauvignon Blanc	d) Loire Valley, France
5. Pinot Noir	e) Rheingau, Germany
6. White Riesling	
7. Sémillon	
8. Chenin Blanc	
9. Petite Sirah (Syrah)	

22. a) What is the most widely planted red-wine grape in California?
b) What is the most widely planted white-wine grape in California?

23. What's unusual about the Alicante Bouschet grape variety?

24. Which grape variety does not belong in the following group?
a) Monterey Riesling
b) Sonoma Riesling
c) Mendocino Riesling
d) White Riesling
e) Franken Riesling

25. Which of the following grape varieties should be omitted from this list?

a) Moscatelle	e) Muscat Ottonel
b) Muscat Canelli	f) Muscat Hamburg
c) Muscat Frontigan	g) Muscadines
d) Muscat Alexandria	h) Black Muscat

i) Muscadet
j) Muscadelle de Bordelais
k) Muscat d'Alsace
l) Orange Muscat

26. Which is which? Match the grape with its description.

1. Napa Gamay
2. Gamay Beaujolais

a) This California grape was believed to be the "true" Gamay of Beaujolais, France. Recently, however, confirmation of an earlier suspicion by a French ampelographer proved that it is actually a lesser variety named Valdiquer.
b) This grape is believed to be a clone of the Pinot Noir that originated from plant stocks at the University of California at Davis, dating back to the 1930s.

27. Which grape is not related to the other two (think carefully)?

a) California White Pinot
b) Pinot Blanc
c) Chenin Blanc

28. In 1981, it was publicly disclosed that the grape variety identified until then as Pinot Blanc in California was actually not the same variety as the "true" Pinot Blanc of Burgundy, but another variety altogether. What grape did the erroneous Pinot Blanc turn out to be?

29. Abundant rainfall at harvest time is:

a) desirable, because it washes the grapes
b) desirable, because it gives the vines a good start for next year's harvest
c) undesirable, because the vines absorb the additional moisture, causing the ripe grapes to swell and diluting their flavor
d) irrelevant, since the grapes are as ripe as they're going to get

30. What is the correct name for the classic white grape of Burgundy, anyway?

a) Chardonnay
b) Pinot Chardonnay
c) both of the above

ANSWERS

1. Vitis *is the genus to which all of the world's grapevines belong.*

2. *a.* Vitis vinifera *was brought to America from Europe by early settlers.*

3. *b.* Vitis labrusca *was just one species found growing wild when the white man arrived; others included* Vitis rupestris, Vitis riparia, *and* Vitis aestivalis, *to name a few.*

4. Vitis vinifera *produces the finest wines of the world. It is this species alone that is used to make the great wines of Bordeaux, Burgundy, and all of Europe. It is the dominant species planted in California and is gaining ground in the eastern United States. Native American vines, such as* labrusca, *tend to yield grapes that are very high in acid and equally low in sugar compared to* vinifera. *In addition, wines produced from* labrusca *grapes have a peculiar aroma and flavor, often referred to as "foxy," which derives from an ester called methyl anthranilate.*

5. *c. grafting. The roots of several native American vine varieties tend to be stronger, more disease-resistant, and more tolerant of frigid winter temperatures than the roots of* vinifera *and many hybrid varieties. It is for this reason that varieties with normally tender roots are grafted onto sturdier American rootstock. The root part of the vine is known as the stock and the grafted part as the scion.*

6. Phylloxera vastatrix, *insects of the Aphididae family, puncture the root cells and suck out the plant juices until the vine dies. Native American vine roots, hard and thick, are resistant to this pest, but the soft, fleshy roots of the* vinifera *species are fatally vulnerable. The only way known to control* phylloxera *is to graft susceptible vines onto native American rootstock.*

It is important to understand that vine roots mainly act as a plumbing system, supplying water and nutrients to the plant; the grafted vines retain their own individual characteristics, and the wines made from these vines are essentially the same as those made from ungrafted vines.

7. *a. hybridization. Enology (sometimes spelled oenology) is the science of winemaking; ampelography refers to the description and identification of grapevines.*

8. *b. They are some of the most famous French hybridizers who developed many of the useful wine grape varieties that eventually found their way to eastern North America.*

9. *Philip Wagner is considered to be the leading pioneer of French-American hybrid varieties in the United States. He established Boordy Vineyard in Riderwood, Maryland, and through his nursery propagated as many as a hundred thousand vines a year, distributing them all over the United States and Canada. In addition, he has written several major books on winemaking and grape growing for amateurs and small growers.*

10. *The De Chaunac, a red hybrid known experimentally as Seibel 9549 (it was developed by Albert Seibel, hence his name preceding the number of the experimental vine), is named in honor of Adhémar De Chaunac, an avid promoter of hybrids and* vinifera *in Canada.*

11. *a, b, c. Eastern American wines have traditionally been made from native grape varieties. However, in the last few decades, wine growers have replanted many vineyards and started new sites with hybrid and* vinifera *varieties, which are producing some excellent dry table wines. Tremendous advances have been made in upgrading the quality of Eastern wines because of these finer varieties. Rieslings and Chardonnays equal to—and, in some cases, better than—those produced in California, Germany, and France are no longer an anomaly. An exciting experience awaits the connoisseur who's been avoiding them because of old-fashioned prejudices.*

12. *1-H, 2-H, 3-N, 4-H, 5-H, 6-V, 7-H, 8-N, 9-H, 10-N, 11-N, 12-N, 13-H, 14-H, 15-V, 16-N, 17-H, 18-V, 19-H, 20-H.*

13. *c. Surprise! Cayuga White, a fine hybrid developed at the Agricultural Experiment Station, Geneva, New York, is a cross be-*

tween Seyval Blanc and Schuyler; Schuyler is a cross between Zinfandel and Ontario. The new variety produces a delightfully light, racy white wine.

14. *b. Three years is the norm.*

15. *False. Too large a quantity usually results in lowered quality. Most vines are carefully pruned in order to control their output.*

16. *False. The best wines come from vines grown on poor soil, thus yielding only modest crops of grapes, which are generally higher in quality.*

17. *b. Four to five tons per acre is a good norm. Generally, young vines produce more fruit and old vines less.*

18. *The amount of wine produced from an acre of vines largely depends upon the yield or tonnage harvested per acre. According to figures compiled by the Virginia Department of Agriculture and Commerce:*
—one ton of grapes makes 200 gallons of juice.
—200 gallons of juice make 180 gallons of wine.
—180 gallons of wine fill 900 bottles, or seventy-five cases.
Thus, one ton of grapes makes approximately seventy-five cases. If the acre produces the average four tons, about three hundred cases of wine could be made.

19. *A limited area within a region that is more suitable to grape growing than its surrounding countryside.*

20. *1–e, 2–d, 3–f, 4–a, 5–b, 6–c, 7–g. It should be pointed out that the first* vinifera *variety, Criolla (later known as Mission), was brought to Baja California from Mexico by Spanish mission fathers in the late 1700s. The vine arrived in Mexico as early as 1524, having been brought there from Spain by the mission fathers. As missions spread through Alta (northern) California, so did the Mission vine. By the 1830s, the missions were in decline, and the vineyards and winemaking had deteriorated. Jean Louis Vignes was the first to import vines and cuttings from Europe; thus, he is considered to be the first grower of* vinifera *varietals in California.*

21. *1–b, 2–a, 3–b, 4–b, and d, 5–a, 6–e, 7–b, 8–d, 9–c.*

22. *a. Zinfandel leads red-wine plantings, with 28,368 acres reported in 1982; Cabernet Sauvignon follows with 22,496 acres.*

b. Colombard, a heavy-bearing vine, is the leader in white-wine varieties, with 56,639 acres reported in 1982; Chenin Blanc follows with 37,421 acres.

23. *Alicante Bouschet is a red grape with red pulp! This characteristic is rare. The few varieties with red pulp are known as* teinturiers, *which comes from the French noun meaning "dyer." Alicante Bouschet is of the* vinifera *species.*

24. *d. White Riesling (aka Johannisberg Riesling) is the "true" noble grape of Germany. The remaining varieties are synonyms for a lesser variety, Sylvaner, which originated in Austria.*

25. *g, i. Muscadines are white and black grape varieties of the species* Vitis rotundifolia *that grow in the southern United States. Muscadet, also known as Melon, is grown in the Loire Valley of France and produces dry, lively white wines also called Muscadet.*
All the other varieties are direct members of the Muscat family.

26. *1–a, 2–b. In November 1981, Charles F. Shaw—who specializes in the production of French Cru-style Beaujolais in the Napa Valley—went to Fleurie and brought back genuine French cuttings for his own vineyard. The "true" Gamay vines now grow on his estate near St. Helena.*

27. *b. Pinot Blanc is a variety unto itself. In California, Chenin Blanc is sometimes called by the misnomer White Pinot. In 1955 the Charles Krug Winery (Napa Valley) was the first to label wines produced from this variety with the correct name, Chenin Blanc.*

28. *Experts identified the purported Pinot Blanc as Melon (*aka *Muscadet), a variety grown primarily in the Loire Valley of France.*

29. *c. Wines produced from grapes exposed to abundant rainfall at harvest time are thin—and rarely, if ever, interesting.*

30. *a. Chardonnay is not a member of the Pinot family and so any reference to Pinot in the name should be dropped once and for all, please.*

FLIGHT II

California

The Pacific Northwest

New York and States East of the Rocky Mountains

Canada

California

The beginning of vine-planting is like the beginning of mining for the precious metals: the wine-grower also prospects. One corner of the land after another is tried with one grape after another. This is a failure; that is better; a third best. So, bit by bit, they grope about for their Clos Vougeot and Lafite. Those lodes and pockets of earth, more precious than the precious ores, that yield inimitable fragrance and soft fire; those virtuous Bonanzas, where the soil has sublimated under sun and stars to something finer, and the wine is bottled poetry . . .

Robert Louis Stevenson
Silverado Squatters

1. Match the following winegrowing counties with the numbered regions on the map.

a) Alameda
b) Amador
c) Mendocino
d) Monterey
e) Napa
f) San Benito
g) San Luis Obispo
h) Santa Clara
i) Santa Cruz
j) Sonoma

2. Potter, Redwood, Ukiah, McDowell, and Anderson are five grape-growing valleys located in:

a) Mendocino County
b) Napa County
c) Lake County
d) Sonoma County

3. Lake County, bordered on the south by Napa, and separated from Mendocino by the Mayacamas Mountains,

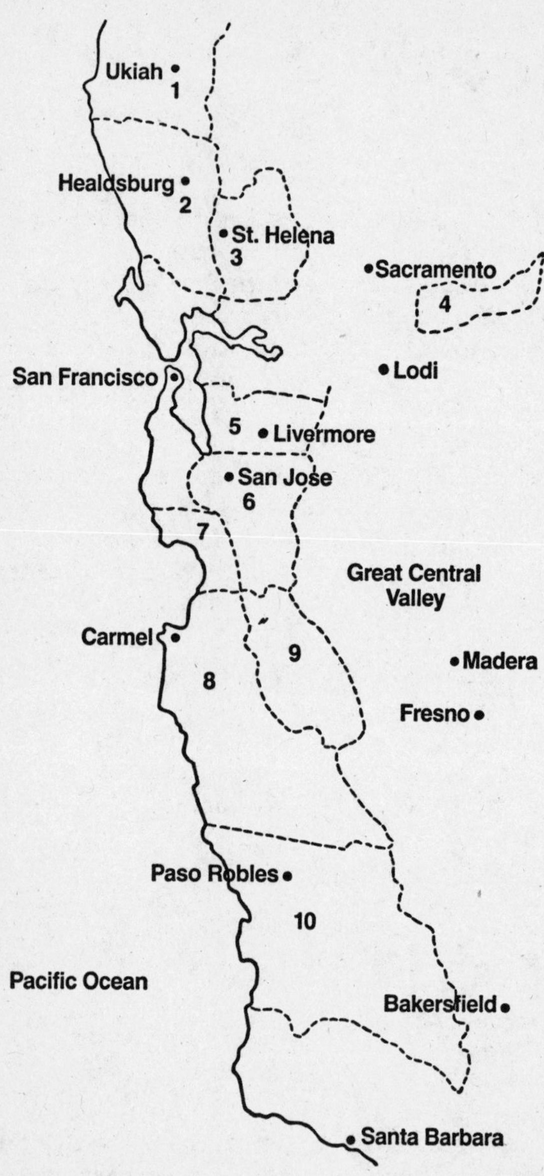
Ukiah
1
Healdsburg
2
St. Helena
3
Sacramento
4
San Francisco
Lodi
5
Livermore
San Jose
6
7
Great Central Valley
Carmel
9
Madera
8
Fresno
Paso Robles
10
Pacific Ocean
Bakersfield
Santa Barbara

benefits from the moderating influence of a large body of water. What is the name of the lake?

4. Which Lake County winery was once owned by the late British actress Lillie Langtry?

5. Which valley does not belong in the following list?
a) Alexander Valley
b) Carmel Valley
c) Dry Creek Valley
d) Russian River Valley
e) Sonoma Valley

6. Which of the valleys listed in Question 5 is also known as the Valley of the Moon?

7. If you wanted to visit the cellars of The Christian Brothers, Inglenook, and Beringer, which valley would you set out for?

8. While sipping a fine Carneros Creek Pinot Noir, you might impress your companions by noting casually that the word *carneros,* in Spanish, means:
a) bull
b) stag
c) sheep
d) bear

9. Anthony Diener was a chemistry teacher before he became cellarmaster of The Christian Brothers wineries in 1936. By what name do wine lovers know him today?

10. Match the following winemakers with the wineries with which they are associated.

1. Richard Arrowood	a) Alexander Valley Vineyards
2. Jerry Luper	b) Chateau Bouchaine
3. Ken Burnap	c) Chateau St. Jean
4. Paul Draper	d) Clos du Val Wine Co.
5. Merry Edwards	e) Dry Creek Vineyard

6. Alison Green	f) Far Niente Winery
7. Zelma Long	g) Firestone Vineyard
8. Gil Nickel	h) Joseph Phelps Vineyards
9. Bernard Portet	i) Matanzas Creek Winery
10. Walter Schug	j) Mayacamas Vineyards
11. David Stare	k) Austin Cellars
12. Robert Travers	l) Ridge Vineyards
13. Anthony Austin	m) Santa Cruz Mountain Vineyard
14. Harry Wetzel III	n) Simi Winery
15. Warren Winiarski	o) Stag's Leap Wine Cellars

11. Which Napa vineyard does not belong in the following list?
a) Lake Vineyard
b) Gravelly Meadow
c) Martha's Vineyard
d) Volcanic Hill
e) Red Rock Terrace

12. What California winery is partially modeled after the Clos de Vougeot château in Burgundy, France?

13. In November 1981, a society was established at Inglenook Vineyards in honor of a particular grape varietal. What is the name of the society and the grape?

14. What is the oldest winery in:
a) Sonoma?
b) Napa?

15. Who is the oldest winegrowing family in the United States?

16. Match the following wineries with their founders:

1. Beaulieu Vineyards	a) Senator Alfred A. Tubbs
2. Buena Vista	b) Pierre Pellier
3. Château Montelena	c) Andrea Sbarboro
4. Cresta Blanca	d) Agoston Haraszthy
5. Hanzell Vineyards	e) Georges de Latour

6. Inglenook	f) Charles Wetmore
7. Italian Swiss Colony	g) Ambassador J. D. Zellerbach
8. Mirassou	h) Gustave Niebaum

17. There were more wineries in Napa Valley prior to Prohibition than in mid-1982. True or false?

18. Name the first viticultural area in California to be given an official designation by the Bureau of Alcohol, Tobacco, and Firearms?

19. The co-proprietors of Château La Mission-Haut-Brion in Bordeaux are minority partners in which Napa winery?

20. What winery derives its name from the fact that in the early 1900s the premises was a frog farm?

21. Amador, Calaveras, and El Dorado are three premium winegrowing counties located in what viticulture area of California?

22. Match the following wineries with their second labels.

1. Caymus Vineyard	a) Falcon Crest
2. Chalone	b) Hawkcrest
3. Louis J. Foppiano	c) Le Fleuron
4. Spring Mountain	d) Gavilan
5. Stag's Leap Wine Cellars	e) Liberty School
	f) Stephens
6. Joseph Phelps	g) Riverside Farm
7. Girard	

23. What is the largest winery in the world?

24. What was the first California winery to:
a) produce a "Nouveau" wine?
b) produce a Blanc de Noirs table wine?
c) bottle Petite Sirah as a varietal wine?
d) label Sauvignon Blanc with the name Fumé Blanc?
e) bottle Merlot as a varietal wine?

25. Which winery does not belong in the following group?

a) Sterling Vineyards
b) The Monterey Vineyard
c) Monterey Peninsula Winery
d) Taylor California Cellars
e) The Taylor Wine Company
f) Great Western Winery

26. At the 1982 World's Fair, held at Knoxville, Tennessee, what wines were designated the official:
a) white pouring wine?
b) red pouring wine?
c) port?

27. Two great wine personalities, one from California, the other from France, made history in 1980 when they announced that they had joined forces to produce a premium Napa Valley Cabernet.
a) Name the two entrepreneurs behind this joint venture.
b) Name the American winemaker and the French winemaker involved in the project.
c) What was the vintage of the first wine produced as a result of this joint venture?

ANSWERS

1. *a–5, b–4, c–1, d–8, e–3, f–9, g–10, h–6, i–7, j–2.*

2. *a. Mendocino County.*

3. *Clear Lake exerts a moderating influence on Lake County vines.*

4. *Guenoc Winery used to be known as the Guenoc Stock Ranch, and was owned by Lillie Langtry. In the 1880s, she hired a Bordeaux wine expert to produce wine from her vineyards and labeled the bottles with her portrait. As a tribute to Langtry, the labels of the current Guenoc winery bear a cameo of the actress.*

5. *b. Carmel Valley lies in Monterey County and is the home of the lovely wine estate Durney Vineyards. The others are all in Sonoma County.*

6. *e. Sonoma Valley is referred to as the Valley of the Moon(s). The American Indians who inhabited the area gave it that name because at night its many hills gave horseback riders the impression that not one, but many moons shined there. The Valley of the Moon was then made famous through the writings of Jack London.*

7. *The Christian Brothers, Inglenook, and Beringer are all located in Napa Valley.*

8. *c. sheep. The label of Carneros Creek wines depicts a ram, the male of the species.*

9. *Brother Timothy is cellarmaster of The Christian Brothers wineries.*

10. *1–c, 2–b, 3–m, 4–l, 5–i, 6–g, 7–n, 8–f, 9–d, 10–h, 11–e, 12–j, 13–k, 14–a, 15–o.*
Note: Zelma Long and her husband, Robert, own their own winery

and vineyards, called Long Vineyards, in Napa Valley. Thus, she is associated with both wineries, her own and Simi.

11. *c. Martha's Vineyard, a forty-acre plot near Oakville, is owned by Tom and Martha May and yields the grapes for Heitz Cellars' most famous Cabernet Sauvignon. The others belong to Al Brounstein, whose sturdy Diamond Creek Cabernets are labeled with these vineyard names.*

12. *The exterior of Hanzell, located in Sonoma County, was built in the 1950s as a replica of part of the famous Clos de Vougeot in Burgundy.*

13. *The Charbono Society, an informal tasting group, was formed in honor of the Charbono grape, which produces a unique red wine of the same name. Less than one hundred acres are planted with this varietal in California, and the wine is produced commercially by only six wineries: Fortino, Franciscan, Inglenook, Papagni, Parducci, and Souverain.*

14. *a. Buena Vista Winery, founded in 1857 by Agoston Haraszthy, is Sonoma's oldest winery.*

b. Charles Krug Winery, established in 1861 by a Prussian emigré for whom it is named, is the oldest in Napa.

15. *The Mirassou family has grown wine grapes continuously since 1854 and began producing wine in 1859. Their impressive establishment, famed for its excellent sparkling wine as well as its fine table wines, is located at San José in Santa Clara County.*

16. *1–e, 2–d, 3–a, 4–f, 5–g, 6–h, 7–c, 8–b.*

17. *True. According to promotional material culled for the 1982 Napa Valley Wine Auction, the record number of Napa wineries is 142, set prior to Prohibition. The count in mid-1982 registered only 135 wineries. Even more interesting is the fact that in 1960 there were only 25 producing wineries.*

18. *Napa Valley was the first area to receive official approval. Beginning in 1983, wine labels and advertising will be able to feature the viticultural area's name if 85 percent of the wine comes from grapes grown within that area.*

19. *Conn Creek Winery.*

20. *Frog's Leap Winery, which is located in Napa Valley, used to* *be a genuine frog farm, selling frogs for 33¢ a dozen. Naturally, its labels depict a leaping frog!*

21. *These counties are located in the rapidly-growing viticultural area known as the Sierra Foothills.*

22. *1–e, 2–d, 3–g, 4–a, 5–b, 6–c, 7–f.*

23. *E. & J. Gallo at Modesto is number one in the world.*

24. *a. In 1972, Sebastiani inaugurated the custom of producing a Nouveau wine—released only weeks after the harvest. Made with Gamay Beaujolais grapes, a clone of Pinot Noir, rather than the fruitier French Gamay, Sebastiani's Nouveau has a different flavor than its prototype.*

b. In 1972, Caymus Vineyards produced the first Blanc de Noirs table wine from Pinot Noir grapes, and christened it Oeil de Perdrix, or Eye of the Partridge.

c. Concannon Vineyard, in Livermore Valley, was the originator of Petite Sirah as a varietal wine. First bottled in 1961 as a non-vintage varietal, the wines were not vintage-dated until 1964.

d. Although the Sauvignon Blanc grape had been grown and used for some time in California, it wasn't very popular until Robert Mondavi introduced wines made from that varietal under the name Fumé Blanc in 1966.

e. In 1972, Louis Martini released the first varietally labeled Merlot, a blend of wines from the 1968 and 1970 vintages.

25. *c. "MPW," as it is known to its admirers, is a separately owned concern. The remaining wineries are all encompassed by The Wine Spectrum, a wholly owned subsidiary of the Coca Cola Company in Atlanta, Georgia.*

26. *a. Wente Bros. 1979 Chardonnay.*

b. Louis M. Martini 1978 Cabernet Sauvignon.

c. Ficklin Port, produced by Ficklin Vineyards of Madera, Calif.

27. *a. Robert Mondavi, whose winery is in Oakville (Napa Valley), and Baron Philippe de Rothschild of Château Mouton-Rothschild (Pauillac).*

b. Tim Mondavi, who is Robert Mondavi's son and winemaker, and Lucien Sionneau, Baron Philippe de Rothschild's winemaker.

c. The first Mondavi-Rothschild wine was produced from the 1979 harvest.

The Pacific Northwest

A Special Grace
Prelude to a feast of wine and food

Once more, Dear Lord, we gather here
To wine and dine, and share good cheer.
May the pinks and whites and Burgundy reds
Enliven our hearts—not lighten our heads!
Give us the grace of moderation
To keep us all in circulation . . .
So we'll enjoy this celebration!

Rev. Charles M. Depiere,
Spokane, Washington

1. In 1980, at a blind tasting of French and American Pinot Noirs organized in Beaune, France, by Burgundian shipper Robert Drouhin, a 1975 Pinot Noir from Oregon took second place, only two-tenths of a point behind a 1959 Chambolle-Musigny, and three points ahead of a 1961 Chambertin-Clos de Bèze. Which winery created this sensation, thereby establishing Oregon as a state with potential for producing great Pinot Noir—a wine that, with few exceptions, has eluded glory in California?

2. Labeling wines with generic names, such as Chablis and Burgundy, is banned in:
   a) Idaho
   b) Oregon
   c) Washington

3. Most of the vineyards in Oregon are located in:
   a) Willamette Valley
   b) Yakima Valley
   c) Umpqua Valley

4. Which was the first post-Prohibition winery to pioneer *vinifera* plantings in Oregon?

5. If you happened to spot a herd of magnificent Roosevelt Elk while winter trekking through Washington County in Oregon, you'd know that you were in the vicinity of which winery, particularly known for its splendid Pinot Noir?

6. What Oregon winery takes its name from a valley situated between Portland and Salem, an extension of the Willamette Valley?

7. If you happened to find a bottle of wine from Oregon labeled "Turkey Wine," you'd know it was a proprietary (brand) name for a delightful, zippy white wine made from a skillful blend of Riesling, Muscat, and Gewürztraminer. Who produces it?

8. What is the largest winery in the Northwest?

9. Which of the following wineries is not located in the state of Washington:
   a) Associated Vintners
   b) Chateau Ste. Michelle
   c) Hinzerling Vineyards
   d) Preston Wine Cellars
   e) Sokol Blosser Winery

10. Washington's two main winegrowing regions, the Columbia River Basin and Yakima Valley, are fenced off from the marine airflow of the Pacific Ocean by the Cascade Mountains, creating a semi-desert climate with hot, sunny days and cool nights during the growing season. True or false?

11. What winery produced Washington State's first commercially available sparkling wine?

12. What Idaho winery is named in honor of the thirteenth-century Gothic chapel on the Ile de la Cité in Paris?

ANSWERS

1. *The 1975 Pinot Noir from Oregon was produced by David Lett at Eyrie Vineyards. Oregon wineries are also producing some excellent Chardonnays and Rieslings which are increasingly being recognized for their fine-tuned quality by connoisseurs the world over.*

2. *b. Oregon has particularly strict labeling laws, and no generic names are permitted, since their use in that state is restricted to imported wines.*

3. *a. Most Oregon vineyards are in Willamette Valley within a forty-five-mile radius south and west of Portland, although a few have been established near Roseburg in the Umpqua Valley. The Yakima Valley is a major grape-growing region in Washington State, not in Oregon.*

4. *Hillcrest Vineyard, near Roseburg, was the first since Prohibition to pioneer* vinifera *in Oregon. In 1961, Richard Sommer, Hillcrest's founder, planted vines from Napa Valley and bonded his winery two years later. A new winery was constructed in 1975, and today Hillcrest produces a wide range of* vinifera *wines including Riesling, Gewürztraminer, and Fumé Blanc, to name a few.*

5. *Elk Cove Vineyards, a small family-owned and -operated concern, is named for the elk, which can be seen during the winter season.*

6. *Tualatin Vineyards takes its name from Tualatin Valley, which is an extension of Willamette Valley. Tualatin was established in 1973 and now has some seventy acres planted in* vinifera *vines, which produce some of Oregon's most delightful wines under the Tualatin Vineyards label.*

7. *Turkey Wine is (occasionally) produced by Knudsen-Erath*

Winery, which is located in Yamhill County, part of the Willamette Valley viticultural area. C. Calvert Knudsen and Richard C. Erath pooled their viticultural resources together in 1975 to form the present winery, which is best known for its fine Pinot Noir, Riesling, Chardonnay, and Gewürztraminer varietal wines.

8. *Chateau Ste. Michelle in the state of Washington is the largest winery in the Northwest.*

9. *e. Sokol Blosser is in Yamhill County, Oregon, and can be added to your list of exceptionally fine wineries in that state.*

10. *True. Washington's grape-growing regions are semiarid; rainfall is sparse, averaging six to fifteen inches per year, depending on the specific location. But there is plenty of water for irrigation, and the complex watering system has turned the area into one of the nation's principal agricultural regions.*

11. *Chateau Ste. Michelle was the first to produce a sparkling wine. In 1982, they released their 1976 Blanc de Noirs, made by the méthode champenoise entirely from Pinot Noir grapes grown in Washington State.*

12. *Ste. Chapelle Vineyards, situated in the Snake River Valley, thirty-five miles west of Boise, was named in honor of the French chapel. The striking new winery has twenty-four-foot-tall narrow stained-glass windows that are replicas of those in Paris. Best-known for its German-style Rieslings made from Idaho grapes grown in the Sunny Slope area, Ste. Chapelle also produces fine Idaho Chardonnay and several wines made from grapes grown in Washington State.*

New York and States East of the Rocky Mountains

Pierce's 1894 Restaurant in Elmira Heights, New York, is renowned not only for its fine food, but also for its extensive wine list. When owner Joe Pierce, Sr., decided that the 1894 Banquet Room needed a new carpet, his wife, Lee, who has a flair for decorating, called in a specialist. Debating over the color of the new carpet, Lee asked the specialist if he had anything available in Burgundy?

"Certainly," he replied, "would you prefer red or white?"

1. What is the oldest winegrowing region in the United States?
2. What viticultural area became America's first official appellation, approved by the Bureau of Alcohol, Tobacco, and Firearms?
3. In the mid-1800s, the foremost winemaking state in America was not California, but one east of the Rocky Mountains. What was that state?
4. Should you encounter table wines labeled Rhode Island Red, America's Cup White, Lighthouse Red, and Compass Rosé, you would know that they were produced by:
   a) Chadwick Bay Wine Company

b) Casa Larga Vineyards
c) Lucas Winery
d) Sakonnet Vineyards

5. Which winery listed in Question 5 is New England's oldest and largest winery?

6. What winery is the largest producer in the eastern United States?

7. What winery has the largest acreage of *vinifera* plantings in the East?

8. Indicate the location of the following New York State wineries as Chautauqua (C), Finger Lakes (F), Hudson Valley (H), or Long Island (L):

1. Bully Hill
2. Glenora Wine Cellars
3. Hargrave Vineyard
4. Plane's Cayuga Vineyard
5. Woodbury Vineyards
6. Johnson (Estate) Vineyards
7. Lenz Vineyards
8. Cascade Mountain Vineyards
9. McGregor Vineyard
10. Wagner Vineyards
11. Hermann J. Wiemer Vineyards
12. Benmarl Wine Company

9. In the left column are names of people with such prominent positions as winemaker or owner at various New York State wineries. Match the names with the wineries.

1. Dr. Konstantin Frank	a) Heron Hill
2. Walter Taylor	b) Gold Seal Vineyards
3. Walter Pedersen	c) Wagner Vineyards
4. Peter Johnstone	d) The Taylor Wine Co.
5. William Wetmore	e) Vinifera Wine Cellars
6. Chris Johnson	f) Clinton Vineyards
7. Guy Devaux	g) Benmarl Wine Co.
8. Ben Feder	h) Cascade Mountain Vineyards
9. Domenic Carisetti	i) Bully Hill
10. Marc Miller	j) Four Chimneys Farm Winery

10. Match the following New England wineries with their states.

1. White Mountain Vineyards	a) Massachusetts
2. Chicama Vineyards	b) New Hampshire
3. Haight Vineyard	c) Rhode Island
4. Commonwealth Winery	d) Connecticut
5. Prudence Island Vineyards	

11. What winery marketed the first commercial *vinifera* wines produced from grapes grown in New York State (in 1960)?

12. What New York State winery estate-bottles under two labels—one depicting a bird and one depicting a beast?

13. In which states are the following wineries located?

1. Banholzer Wine Cellars
2. Montbray Wine Cellars
3. Gross' Highland Winery
4. Wiederkehr Wine Cellars
5. Canandaigua Wine Co.
6. Possum Trot Vineyards
7. Markko Vineyard
8. Fenn Valley Vineyards
9. Meredyth Vineyard
10. Mount Hope Estate
11. Tabor Hill
12. Renault Winery
13. Widmer's Wine Cellars
14. Nissley Vineyards
15. La Buena Vida Vineyards
16. Wollersheim Winery
17. Château Lagniappe
18. Chadds Ford Winery
19. The Biltmore Company
20. Château Elan

14. What is the name of the largest winery in Ohio?

15. What well-known Italian wine firm purchased an 850-acre farm in Barboursville, Virginia in 1976 and has since developed a *vinifera* vineyard on part of the site?

ANSWERS

1. *The Hudson Valley in New York State is the oldest winegrowing region in America. Wine has been made along the Hudson River since French Huguenots settled the town of New Paltz in 1677. The first commercial winery opened at Croton Point in 1827, and the oldest active winery in the United States is located at Washingtonville, established in 1839 and now operating as the Brotherhood Winery.*

2. *Augusta County, Virginia became America's first official appellation.*

3. *By 1858, Cincinnati wineries had made Ohio the leading wine state of the country, producing more than a third of the national total. Leon Adams mentions in his book* The Wines of America *that there were 161 wineries in Ohio in 1937. Wine production there never fully recovered after Prohibition, but Ohio in 1982 contained about 39 prospering wineries.*

4. *d. Sakonnet Vineyards is located in Rhode Island and produces some excellent table wines from both* vinifera *and hybrid varieties. The other wineries are all located in New York State.*

5. *White Mountain Vineyards, founded at Laconia, New Hampshire, in 1969, is New England's oldest and largest winery; it controls about 174 acres of vines and has a storage capacity of eighty-five thousand gallons. Their table wines are produced from many different grape varieties, predominantly the French-American hybrids, which grow well in the sandy New Hampshire soil.*

6. *The Taylor Wine Company of Hammondsport, New York, founded in 1880 on a seven-acre plot of vineyards, has grown dramatically to become the largest producer of wines in the eastern United States. In 1961, The Taylor Wine Company acquired the Pleasant Valley Wine Company (Great Western), which greatly in-*

creased its size. Since its merger with The Coca Cola Company in 1977, capital infusion into Taylor has upgraded and expanded production facilities so that grape crushing capacity now exceeds 1,000 tons per day and wine storage capacity totals 23,862,000 gallons. Taylor is part of The Wine Spectrum, which is the third largest wine company in the United States.

7. *Gold Seal Vineyards of Hammondsport, New York, has the largest acreage of* vinifera *plantings in the East, with nearly 150 acres, mostly planted on the hospitable shores of Seneca Lake.*

8. *1–F, 2–F, 3–L, 4–F, 5–C, 6–C, 7–L, 8–H, 9–F, 10–F, 11–F, 12–H.*

9. *1–e, 2–i, 3–j, 4–a, 5–h, 6–c, 7–b, 8–f, 9–d, 10–g.*

10. *1–b, 2–a, 3–d, 4–a, 5–c.*

11. *Gold Seal Vineyards, in 1960, was the first winery to market* vinifera *wines made from grapes grown in New York State. The grapes included Chardonnay, Pinot Noir, Gamay, and Johannisberg Riesling.*

12. *Heron Hill Vineyards of Hammondsport, New York, estate-bottles their wines under the Heron Hill label and the Otter Springs label. Both labels were designed by partner and winemaker Peter Johnstone and are a tribute to his talents.*

13. *1–Indiana, 2–Maryland, 3–New Jersey, 4–Arkansas, 5–New York, 6–Indiana, 7–Ohio, 8–Michigan, 9–Virginia, 10–Pennsylvania, 11–Michigan, 12–New Jersey, 13–New York, 14–Pennsylvania, 15–Texas, 16–Wisconsin, 17–Ohio, 18–Pennsylvania, 19–North Carolina, 20–Georgia.*

14. *Meier's Wine Cellars at Cincinnati, founded in 1895, is the largest winery in Ohio.*

15. *Cantine Zonin acquired the Barboursville tract that had once been the plantation of Virginia Governor James Barbour. They chose Virginia for their venture because its climate closely resembles Zonin's vineyard sites in the Veneto. As of this writing, approximately twenty-five acres have been cultivated with* vinifera *vines.*

Canada

The best kind of wine is that which is most pleasant to him who drinks it.

Pliny the Elder

1. The Niagara Peninsula of Ontario and the Okanagan Valley make up the chief winegrowing areas of Canada. Which of the two areas produces 75 percent of all Canadian wines?
2. Some of the wines produced in Canada are made from imported grapes or juice, or a blend of Canadian and imported grapes, but all of the wines produced in Ontario are made from grapes grown in Ontario. True or false?
3. What is the approximate acreage of vineyards in Ontario?
   a) 25,000
   b) 50,000
   c) 75,000
   d) 100,000
4. For an Ontario wine to be labeled varietally, the percentage of that grape variety that it must contain is:
   a) 51
   b) 75
   c) 85
   d) 100
5. Who started the first commercial vineyard and winery in Ontario in 1811?
   a) Maurice Baco
   b) Oliver (Ollie) Bradt

c) Johann Schiller
d) Thomas Bright

6. What is the name of the oldest existing wine company in Ontario?
a) T. G. Bright & Co., Ltd.
b) Barnes Wines Ltd.
c) Inniskillin House Wines Inc.
d) Château-Gai Wines Ltd.

7. What was the previous name of the wine company known today as T. G. Bright & Co., Ltd.?

8. Ontario Superior is a designation reserved for wines that adhere to set standards and meet the approval of an official tasting committee. Which of the following is *not* a requirement for still table wines seeking the Superior designation?
a) must be made entirely from fresh hybrid or vinifera grapes
b) must not exceed 13% alcohol by volume
c) no alcohol may be added by volume
d) must be aged at least three years with a minimum of 51% of the blend aged in small oak casks
e) must have a cork closure

ANSWERS

1. *Ontario produces three-quarters of all Canadian wines.*

2. *True.*

3. *a. 25,000 acres.*

4. *b. 75 percent.*

5. *c. Johann Schiller.*

6. *b. Barnes Wines Limited, originally called the Ontario Grape Growing and Wine Manufacturing Co., Ltd., began in 1873 at St. Catharines and is still operating today.*

7. *Bright's was previously called The Niagara Falls Wine Company. After the death of its founder, Thomas Bright, its name was changed to T. G. Bright & Co., Ltd.*

8. *d. There are no aging requirements for still table wines. The aging requirements described apply only to dessert wines seeking the Superior designation.*

FLIGHT III

Bordeaux
Burgundy
Côtes du Rhône
Alsace
The Loire

Bordeaux

Pour éloigner l'heure du trepas, buvez Médoc à tout repas.
(To postpone the hour of death, drink Médoc at every meal.)

A sign posted at Château Belgrave,
Fifth Growth, Saint Laurent

1. Bordeaux produces:
   a) Red wines only
   b) White wines only
   c) Both red and white wines
2. Which of the following is not an important wine district in Bordeaux?
   a) Sauternes
   b) Graves
   c) Médoc
   d) Lafite
   e) Saint-Émilion
   f) Pomerol
3. Name the four most important communes in the Médoc district.
4. In which department is the Bordeaux wine region located?
   a) Garonne
   b) Gironde
   c) Dordogne
5. Which one of the following grape varieties would not be found in a red wine from Bordeaux?
   a) Cabernet Franc
   b) Cabernet Sauvignon
   c) Pinot Noir
   d) Merlot
   e) Petit Verdot
   f) Malbec
6. In the Médoc, which of the grapes listed in Question 5 is the dominant variety?

7. In Saint-Émilion and Pomerol, which of the grapes listed in Question 5 is the dominant variety?

8. Which one of the following grape varieties would not be found in a white wine from Bordeaux:
   a) Chardonnay
   b) Sauvignon Blanc
   c) Merlot Blanc
   d) Sémillon
   e) Muscadelle

9. Which of the following is not a district in Bordeaux:
   a) Côtes de Bourg
   b) Côtes de Blaye
   c) Côtes de Provence
   d) Entre-Deux-Mers

10. What is the difference between claret and red Bordeaux?

11. Number the following Bordeaux appellations in ascending order of importance, with (#1) as the most basic designation:
    Bordeaux Supérieur
    Château Margaux
    Médoc
    Margaux
    Bordeaux
    Haut-Médoc

12. The word *supérieur,* as in Bordeaux Supérieur, indicates that a wine is of superior quality. True or false?

13. How do you know when a Bordeaux wine has been château-bottled?

14. If a wine is château-bottled, you are guaranteed of its authenticity, but not necessarily of its quality. True or false?

15. Aside from the literal translation, what are *petits châteaux?*

16. What is a *chai?*
    a) an underground storage area
    b) a property that makes wine
    c) a ground-level storage area
    d) a wooden bowl used for beating egg whites when fining

17. Approximately how much wine does a *barrique* (small oak barrel) hold?
a) 10 gallons
b) 25 gallons
c) 55 gallons
d) 100 gallons

18. What is the Classification of 1855?

19. In the original Classification of 1855, which four great châteaux were ranked as Premiers Crus (first growths)?

20. What great château protested against its placement as a second growth in the Classification of 1855 and was finally elevated to first-growth status in 1973?

21. What château now heads the list of second growths in the Classification of 1855?

22. How are the wines listed within the categories of the Classification of 1855?
a) alphabetically
b) geographically by commune
c) presumed order of merit

23. When the vineyards of Saint-Émilion were finally classified in 1955, which two were designated as the leading properties?

24. Which important wine district in Bordeaux has no official classification?

25. Château Desmirail, ranked as a third growth in 1855, has been absorbed by another third-growth property; which one?

26. In which year was it established that a wine from the commune of Cantenac could use the appellation Margaux?
a) 1855
b) 1953
c) 1955
d) 1966

27. Which commune in the Haut-Médoc has three Premiers Crus within its boundaries?

28. a) What was the previous name of Château Mouton Baronne Philippe?
b) What was the original name of this château?

29. Domaine de Balardin is used as a second label by two third-growth Margaux properties that are under mutual ownership. Domaine de Balardin is a blend of wines from both properties; what are their names?

30. Match the following "second labels" with their appropriate Bordeaux producers:

1. Les Forts de Latour	a) Château Gloria
2. Moulin de Duhart	b) Château Cos d'Estournel
3. Moulin des Carruades	c) Château Latour
4. Château Notton	d) Château Beychevelle
5. Domaine des Gondats	e) Château Lafite-Rothschild
6. Château Peymartin	f) Château Brane-Cantenac
7. Clos du Marquis	g) Château Croizet-Bages
8. Château de Marbuzet	h) Château Duhart-Milon-Rothschild
9. Clos de l'Admiral	i) Château Léoville-Las-Cases
10. Enclos de Moncabon	j) Château Marquis-de-Terme

31. What artist was featured on the label of 1973 Château Mouton-Rothschild, and what was especially significant about that particular year?

32. The motto *"Le Roi des Vins—Le Vin des Rois"* (King of Wines—Wine of Kings) can be found on the label of what second-growth Bordeaux?

33. a) What is the name of the white wine produced at Château Margaux?

b) What was the name of Château Margaux in the fifteenth century?

34. What is the name of the white wine produced at Château Talbot?

35. What is the name of the rosé wine produced at Château Lascombes?

36. Who, known as the "Vine Prince" in the eighteenth century, is reputed to have said, "I make wine at Lafite and Latour, but my heart is at Calon"?

37. What château is guarded by stone lions and has as its motto, *"Suis le lion qui ne mord point sinon quand l'ennemi me poing"* (I am the lion who only attacks when I am attacked)?

38. What is the only important district in Bordeaux where many classified properties make both red and white wines?

39. The Graves district is so named because:
a) the area was once a Roman burial ground
b) the people of the area take their wine seriously
c) the soil in the area contains a lot of gravel and sand
d) the wines of the area are so dry that no one can smile when they drink them

40. Which was the only Graves to be included among the Crus Classés in the Classification of 1855?

41. Which of the following wines is not produced in Graves?
a) Château Bouscaut
b) Chateau St. Jean
c) Château Carbonnieux
d) Château de Fieuzal

42. How can one tell from the label if a white Graves is dry or more likely to be off-dry?

43. White Graves wines must be drunk young and do not age well. True or false?

44. What is the name of the white wine produced by Château La Mission-Haut-Brion?

45. Which is the rarest of all white Graves?

46. Appellation Contrôlée Sauternes can be either dry or sweet. True or false?

47. What is the name of the dry white wine occasionally produced at Château d'Yquem?

48. Why do many vineyards in Bordeaux and elsewhere have roses planted at the end of each vineyard row?

49. If you come across a red Bordeaux labeled Cabernet Sauvignon, you should know immediately that it is:
a) a fraud; wines are not allowed to be named after grape varieties in Bordeaux
b) probably only 75 percent Cabernet Sauvignon, since all Bordeaux wines must be blended by law
c) one of the finest wines of the region, since Cabernet Sauvignon is the noblest red-grape variety
d) made from 100 percent Cabernet Sauvignon

ANSWERS

1. c. *Both red and white wines are produced in Bordeaux.*

2. d. *Lafite is a Premier Cru within the Médoc.*

3. *Paulliac, Margaux, Saint-Estèphe, and Saint-Julien are the four most important communes in the Médoc.*

4. b. *Gironde.*

5. c. *Pinot Noir is the leading red-grape variety of Burgundy.*

6. b. *Cabernet Sauvignon is the dominant grape variety in the Médoc.*

7. d. *Merlot is the dominant grape variety in Saint-Émilion and Pomerol.*

8. a. *Chardonnay is the leading white variety of Burgundy.*

9. c. *Côtes de Provence is a vineyard area in southern France near the Mediterranean Sea.*

10. *The terms are synonymous where French wines are concerned. The word claret originated in England from the medieval word* clairet, *and it is commonly used in English-speaking countries to designate the red wines of Bordeaux.*

11. *1–Bordeaux, 2–Bordeaux Supérieur, 3–Médoc, 4–Haut-Médoc, 5–Margaux, 6–Château Margaux.*

12. *False. The word is not an indication of superior quality. "Supérieur" simply means that wines labeled as such contain 1 percent more alcohol than those labeled just "Bordeaux."*

13. *If a wine is château-bottled, this will be indicated on the label by the phrase* mis en bouteille au château.

14. *True. Any property can bottle its own wine, regardless of the* *quality, and state on the label that it is* mis en bouteille au château. *Château-bottling is not reserved for just the best wines, nor is it true that a wine is of poorer quality if it is not château-bottled.*

15. *The term* petits châteaux *refers to the many small vineyards that have not been classified. These are the lesser properties in Bordeaux, which often provide charming, everyday drinking wines at affordable prices.*

16. *c. ground-level storage area.*

17. *c. fifty-five gallons, or twenty-four cases of wine.*

18. *In 1855, in preparation for the Paris Exposition of that year, a committee of experts and wine brokers officially classified the leading wines of Bordeaux. Their ratings were based on the prices and opinions then prevailing. Sixty wines of the Médoc, one Graves, and twenty-two Sauternes were classified as the elite of the region.*

19. *Château Lafite, Château Margaux, Château Latour, and Château Haut-Brion were ranked in that order as Premiers Crus in the Classification of 1855.*

20. *Château Mouton-Rothschild protested against its rank as a second growth and took the motto,* "Premier nu puis, second ne daigne, Mouton suis" *(First I cannot be, second I will not be, I am Mouton). When Mouton was finally elevated to a Premier Cru in 1973, Baron Philippe changed the motto as follows:* "Premier je suis, second je fus, Mouton ne change!" *(First I am, second I have been, Mouton remains the same!)*

21. *Château Rausan-Ségla now heads the list of second growths.*

22. *c. presumed order of merit.*

23. *Château Ausone and Château Cheval Blanc were ranked as the two leading properties in the 1955 classification of Saint-Émilion.*

24. *Pomerol has never been officially classified. Unofficially, Château Pétrus is ranked as Pomerol's best, and some connoisseurs place it on a par with the Premier Crus of the Médoc.*

25. *Château Desmirail was purchased by Château Palmer in 1957 and added to the Palmer vineyard holdings.*

26. *d. 1966.*

27. *Pauillac is the home of three Premier Crus: Château Lafite-Rothschild, Château Latour, and Château Mouton-Rothschild.*

28. *a. Château Mouton Baronne Philippe was previously known as Château Mouton Baron Philippe. Baron Philippe de Rothschild changed the name in 1975 to honor his late wife.*
b. Until 1956 it was called Château Mouton de'Armailhacq.

29. *Château Malescot-Saint Exupéry and Château Marquis-d'Alesme-Becker blend their lesser-quality wines together and sell them as Domaine de Balardin.*

30. *1–c, 2–h, 3–e, 4–f, 5–j, 6–a, 7–i, 8–b, 9–d, 10–g.*

31. *Picasso was featured on the 1973 label of Mouton-Rothschild. It's interesting to note that 1973 was the year that Picasso died, and it's also the year that Mouton was elevated to Premier Cru status.*

32. *Château Gruaud-Larose, second growth, Saint-Julien, uses this motto on its label.*

33. *a) The small amount of white wine produced at Château Margaux is called Pavillon-Blanc de Château Margaux.*
b) In the twelfth century, Château Margaux was named La Mott or Lamothe. The current Château Lamothe, a Premières Côtes de Bordeaux, is not related.

34. *Talbot produces a small amount of white wine known as Caillou-Blanc du Château Talbot.*

35. *Chevalier de Lascombes is the name of the rosé produced by Château Lascombes. It is sold in a slender, clear bottle with the appellation Bordeaux Supérieur.*

36. *This statement was supposedly made by the Marquis Alexandre de Ségur who once owned Lafite, Latour, and Calon-Ségur. A heart shown on the label of Calon-Ségur commemorates his fondness for this property.*

37. *This is the motto of Château Leoville-las-Cases, second growth, Saint-Julien.*

38. *Graves is the only important district in Bordeaux where most classified properties make both red and white wines.*

39. *c. The soil in the area contains a lot of gravel and sand.*

40. *Château Haut-Brion in the commune of Pessac was the only Graves included among the Crus Classés in 1855.*

41. *b. Chateau St. Jean is a winery in Kenwood (Sonoma), California.*

42. *Wines labeled with the Graves appellation are dry; those labeled Graves Supérieurs have 1* percent *more alcohol and are often off-dry because riper grapes are used in their production.*

43. *False. Good white Graves can be enjoyed young or old. Properly stored, the better-quality white Graves can improve over several years. With age, the rounder, richer flavor of the Sémillon surmounts the aggressive character of the Sauvignon Blanc, which dominates in a young wine.*

44. *Laville Haut-Brion is the white wine produced at Château La Mission Haut Brion.*

45. *Pape Clément Blanc is so rare that few people realize it exists. The vineyard, planted with half Sémillon and half Sauvignon Blanc, covers less than an acre; fewer than one hundred cases of white wine are produced each year.*

46. *False. Sauternes is always a sweet wine. If a producer in Sauternes wishes to make a dry wine, it can only be sold as Bordeaux Blanc.*

47. *Made primarily with Sauvignon Blanc, the dry white wine occasionally produced at Château d'Yquem is labeled Château Y (pronounced "ee-greck").*

48. *Roses are more susceptible to mildew than grape vines; when mildew appears on the roses, the growers know that it's time to spray the vines.*

49. *d. Made from 100 percent Cabernet Sauvignon, according to French law.*

Burgundy

Magnificent, with a penetrating bouquet of violets, mingling with a perfume of cherries, the color of sparkling rubies and an extremely delicate softness.

Dr. Ramain
on Romanée-Conti

A white wine of great bearing, rich in alcohol, forceful, golden, sappy, smelling of cinnamon and tasting of gun flint.

Camille Rodier
on Corton-Charlemagne

1. Can you name the four departments that comprise the wine-producing area of Burgundy?
2. Name the two red-grape varieties that are grown in the Burgundy District.
3. What grape has borrowed its name from a hamlet lying in the vicinity of Puligny-Montrachet?
4. What is Passe-Tout-Grains?
5. What is the local name given to the Chardonnay grape in the Chablis area?
6. Name the four appellations of Chablis.
7. How many Grand Cru (great growth) vineyards are there in Chablis? Can you name them?
8. What are the three significant levels of quality in the Côte d'Or?

9. How many Grand Cru vineyards are there in the Côte d'Or?

10. In the Côte de Nuits, what is the only Grand Cru vineyard that produces a white wine?

11. In the Côte de Beaune, what is the only Grand Cru vineyard that produces a red wine?

12. What is the largest vineyard in Burgundy?

13. Which phrase indicates that a Burgundy was "estate-bottled"?
   a) mis en bouteille au domaine
   b) mis en bouteille à la propriété
   c) mis au domaine
   d) all of the above

14. What is the Hospices de Beaune?

15. Which name does not belong in the following group?
   a. Montrachet
   b. Bâtard-Montrachet
   c. Puligny-Montrachet
   d. Chevalier-Montrachet
   e. Bienvenue-Bâtard-Montrachet

16. Match each wine listed below with the letter of the *smallest* Appellation Contrôlée area that it is entitled to use.

1. Les Musigny	a) Bourgogne
2. Romanée-Conti	b) Clos de Vougeot
3. Les Richebourg	c) Vosne-Romanée
4. Chambertin	d) Romanée-Conti
5. Bourgogne Rouge	e) Musigny
6. Les Fèves	f) Chablis
7. Chablis Vaillons	g) Chablis Premier Cru
8. Clos Vougeot	h) Chambolle-Musigny
	i) Chambertin
	j) Gevrey-Chambertin
	k) Richebourg
	l) Beaune

17. What do the names Rully, Mercurey, Givry, and Montagny have in common?

18. Which vineyard does not belong in the following group?

a) La Tâche	e) Richebourg
b) Romanée Saint-Vivant	f) La Romanée
c) Échézeaux	g) Romanée-Conti
d) Grands Échézeaux	h) Montrachet

The fine and almost fine Beaujolais wines are delicate, light and sappy. Though they are not so rich in bouquet as the great wines of Upper Burgundy, they do not lack fragrance. They are, in general, not deeply colored; or, to be more accurate, they settle quickly and come rapidly to maturity. Precociousness is one of their main features.

Victor Rendu

19. All Beaujolais wine is red. True or false?

20. What are the three major appellations of Beaujolais?

21. How many villages are entitled to use the appellation Beaujolais-Villages?

22. How many of the nine Crus Beaujolais can you name?

23. Of the Crus, which is called the king of Beaujolais and which the queen?

24. Which Cru Beaujolais is the farthest north and which is the farthest south?

25. What grape variety is used to produce the red wines of Beaujolais?

26. What white-grape varieties are grown in Beaujolais?

27. What special method is used to vinify red Beaujolais?

28. What is the significance of the white lilies that flourish in the vineyards of Beaujolais?

29. What is Beaujolais Nouveau, or Primeur, as it is sometimes called?

ANSWERS

1. *In a decree dated April 29, 1930, the Civil Tribunal of Dijon defined Burgundy wine production areas as follows: "Local, consistent and time-honored usage has it that the Burgundy wine area is exclusively composed of the Côte d'Or, Yonne and Saône-et-Loire departments, plus the Villefranche-sur-Saône arrondissement in the Rhône department."*

The Côte d'Or, known as the "slope of gold," is considered the heart of Burgundy. It is divided into two sections: the Côte de Nuits, to the north, famous for its superb red wines; and the Côte de Beaune, to the south, renowned for its magnificent white wines, although it produces more red than white.

The Yonne is the northernmost department of Burgundy and contains the commune of Chablis, which produces probably the best-known and most imitated dry white wine in the world.

The Department of the Saône-et-Loire lies directly south of the Côte d'Or and includes the Côte Chalonnaise, the Mâconnais, and a small part of Beaujolais.

The Department of the Rhône includes the vast majority of the Beaujolais communes and vineyards. (It should not be confused with the large wine-producing area farther south called Côtes du Rhône.)

2. *The noble grape, Pinot Noir, produces the red wines of the Côte d'Or. The Gamay, better suited to southern Burgundy, is used in Beaujolais and the Mâconnais.*

3. *The Gamay grape is named after a hamlet located just west of Puligny-Montrachet.*

4. *Red wines that are made by vatting Pinot Noir and Gamay grapes together are labeled Bourgogne Passe-Tout-Grains. They are pleasant, light wines and are usually inexpensive.*

5. *In Chablis, the Chardonnay grape is often called the Beaunois, meaning "plant of Beaune." It is thought that Chardonnay was introduced to the Chablis area in the twelfth century by monks who came from the Côte d'Or, where Chardonnay dominates white wine production, specifically in the Côte de Beaune—hence the name, Beaunois.*

6. *Chablis Grand Cru—these are the elite vineyards of Chablis, and the labels of these wines proudly show their Grand Cru status.*

Chablis Premier Cru—twenty-nine vineyards that are considered only slightly inferior to the Grands Crus are permitted to use this appellation.

Chablis—this is a blend of wines from several vineyards and accounts for about half the production of the area.

Petit Chablis—wines with this appellation come from the outer parts of the district. They are lighter-bodied wines, but can be attractive if consumed in their youth.

7. *The most elegant wines of Chablis come from its seven Grand Cru vineyards: Les Clos, Blanchots, Bougros, Valmur, Vaudésir, Les Preuses, and Grenouilles.*

8. *The three significant levels of quality in the Côte d'Or are: Grands Crus, Premiers Crus, and village wines. Although there has never been an official classification of the Côte d'Or vineyards similar to the 1855 Bordeaux Classification, the above rating system has been incorporated into the official "Appellation Contrôlée" laws of Burgundy, based on time-honored tradition and analysis of each vineyard.*

9. *Thirty-one vineyards have been rated as Grands Crus in the Côte d'Or. Twenty-four of them are in the Côte de Nuits, twenty-three producing red wines, and only one producing a white wine. The Côte de Beaune has seven Grand Cru vineyards, six of which produce white wines and only one of which produces a red.*

10. *Musigny Blanc is the only Grand Cru white wine in the Côte de Nuits. However, the quantity produced is so small that it is rarely available.*

11. *Le Corton, which lies in the commune of Aloxe-Corton, is the only Grand Cru vineyard that produces a red wine in the Côte de Beaune.*

12. *Clos de Vougeot is the largest vineyard in Burgundy and at present consists of 124 acres. Although it is a single vineyard, its ownership is shared by over eighty proprietors, each with his own parcel of vines. Naturally, a vineyard with so many owners produces wines of varying quality, depending on the skill of each individual proprietor.*

13. *d. The label of an estate-bottled Burgundy could show any one of the three phrases.*

14. *The Hospices de Beaune is a charitable hospital that was founded in the fifteenth century by Nicolas Rolin, chancellor to Duke Philip the Good of Burgundy. Many vineyard parcels have been bequeathed to the hospital, and the wines made from these vineyards are auctioned off annually on the third Sunday in November. The proceeds go to support the hospital. Although the wines are very good Burgundies, they are usually overpriced for the sake of this worthy charity.*

15. *c. Puligny-Montrachet is a commune in the Côte de Beaune. The other names are all vineyards located, wholly or in part, within the commune of Puligny-Montrachet.*

16. *1–e, 2–d, 3–k, 4–i, 5–a, 6–l, 7–g, 8–b.*

17. *They are all controlled appellations in the Côte Chalonnaise.*

18. *f. La Romanée is a privately owned vineyard. All the others are wholly or in part owned or controlled by the Domaine de la Romanée-Conti.*

19. *False. Most Beaujolais is red wine, but a very small amount of white wine, called Beaujolais Blanc, is also made in the area.*

20. *Cru Beaujolais, Beaujolais-Villages, and Beaujolais are the three major appellations. Cru Beaujolais, the finest wines of the region, are produced from vineyards in nine designated areas (not necessarily villages) located in the northern part of the district. Beaujolais-Villages comes from thirty additional communes near the Crus, and plain Beaujolais from the remainder of the district to the south.*

21. *Thirty-nine villages, including the Cru communes wholly or in part, are entitled to use the appellation Beaujolais-Villages. Naturally, a Cru would not use this lesser designation except in unusual circumstances—overproduction, for example. Following is a list of the communes as they appear in the Beaujolais Décret of September 1937:*

Department of the Rhône: Juliénas, Jullié, Emeringes, Chenas, Fleurie, Chiroubles, Lancié, Villié-Morgon, Lantigné, Beaujeu, Régnié, Durette, Cercié, Quincié, Saint-Lager, Odenas, Charentay, Saint-Etienne-la-Varenne, Vaux, Le Perréon, Saint-Etienne-des-Ouillières, Blacé, Arbuissonnas, Salles, Saint-Julien, Montmelas, Rivolet, Denice, Les Ardillats, Marchampt, Vauxrenard.

Department of Saône-et-Loire: Leynes, Saint-Amour-Bellevue, La Chapelle-de-Guinchay, Romanèche, Pruzilly, Chânes, Saint-Veran, Saint-Symphorien-d'Ancelles.
Note: Occasionally, one of the above village names will appear on the label together with the word Beaujolais, but more often the wine will be labeled simply as Beaujolais-Villages.

22. *Brouilly, Côte-de-Brouilly, Chénas, Chiroubles, Juliénas, Fleurie, Morgon, St. Amour, and Moulin-à-Vent make up the nine Crus Beaujolais.*

23. *Moulin-à-Vent is the king of Beaujolais; Fleurie is the queen.*

24. *Saint-Amour, whose name means holy love, is the northernmost cru; Brouilly is the southernmost.*

25. *The grapes used in red Beaujolais are from the Gamay family, which includes over twenty-five Gamay varieties. The Gamay Geoffray is the most widely used.*

26. *Chardonnay, Aligoté, and Gamay Blanc are all grown in Beaujolais. By law, up to 15 percent of the wine in the area may be made from white varieties.*

27. *If you guessed carbonic maceration or whole berry fermentation, you are partially correct. Actually, Beaujolais is vinified by a combination of traditional and carbonic maceration fermentations. In this method, whole bunches of grapes, including stems and stalks, are placed into closed vats. The grapes at the bottom are nat-*

urally squashed from the weight of those above. Fermentation begins at the bottom of the tank, when the leaking juices come in contact with the yeast on the skins. The natural fermentation process gives off carbon dioxide (carbonic gas), which rises to the top of the vat, surrounding the berries in its path—hence the name carbonic maceration. The gas causes the unbroken grapes to ferment within their skins in the absence of air. Eventually, all the grapes break, and the must finalizes its fermentation in the traditional way. The wine is pressed only after fermentation is complete.

28. *Growers in Beaujolais predict that the harvest will begin three months after the lilies bloom.*

29. *Beaujolais Nouveau, also called Primeur, is literally the first wine of the harvest, fermented for only a short period of time to produce a very light, fruity, quaffing wine that is rather delicate. Because it has a minimum amount of tannin, its lifespan is generally only a few months long, although in exceptional vintages the wine can be enjoyable for up to a year. November 15 is the legal date that the wines can be released for sale, just weeks after the harvest.*

Côtes du Rhône

1. The Côtes du Rhône region is divided into two distinct districts; what are they?
   a) Languedoc and Roussillon
   b) Provence and Midi
   c) the northern Rhône and the southern Rhône
   d) the eastern Rhône and the western Rhône
2. Which district produces the finest wines of the Rhône?
3. Which soil element is characteristic of the vineyards of the Côtes du Rhône?
   a) granite
   b) sand
   c) chalk
   d) clay
4. Red wines of the Rhône generally tend to be softer and lighter than those of Burgundy. True or false?
5. Which is the dominant grape variety of the Côtes du Rhône?
   a) Carignan
   b) Syrah
   c) Grenache
   d) Cinsault
6. Which grape variety listed in Question 5 is used in all red wines from the northern Rhône?
7. Which of the following white-grape varieties would not be found in a wine from the Rhône:
   a) Viognier
   b) Roussanne

c) Chenin Blanc
d) Marsanne

8. In the Côtes du Rhône, white-grape varieties are used both for making white wines and for softening some of the red wines. True or false?

9. How many different grape varieties may be used in the production of red wines labeled Châteauneuf-du-Pape?

10. If you find a bottle of red wine labeled Côtes du Rhône, you should immediately know that it is:
a) one of the best wines of the northern Rhône
b) a regional blend of the area
c) made entirely from the Syrah grape variety
d) a fake; only white wines can be labeled Côtes du Rhône

11. Which commune is famous for its magnificent, fruity white wines produced from the Viognier grape variety?
a) Cornas
b) Saint-Joseph
c) Gigondas
d) Condrieu

12. Château Grillet is France's smallest appellation contrôlée area. True or false?

ANSWERS

1. *c. the northern Rhône and the southern Rhône.*

2. *The finest wines are produced in the northern Rhône, notably at Côte Rôtie, Hermitage, Crozes-Hermitage, Cornas, Saint-Joseph, Château Grillet, and Condrieu.*

3. *a. granite.*

4. *False. The growing season in the Côtes du Rhône is long and hot, generally creating red wines that are more robust and alcoholic than those of Burgundy.*

5. *c. Grenache is the dominant grape variety of the Côtes du Rhône.*

6. *b. Syrah is used in all red wines from the northern Rhône.*

7. *c. Chenin Blanc is the dominant grape variety of the lower Loire Valley.*

8. *True. The best-known example of a red wine produced from both red and white grape varieties is Châteauneuf-du-Pape.*

9. *Up to thirteen different grape varieties, red and white, may be used in making the red wines of Châteauneuf-du-Pape.*

10. *b. a regional blend of the area.*

11. *d. Condrieu is famous for its wonderful white wines.*

12. *False. La Romanée, a 2-acre Grand Cru in Burgundy's Côte de Nuits, is the smallest appellation contrôlée area. Château Grillet, with 3.5 acres, is the second smallest area.*

Alsace

1. Only white wines are produced in Alsace. True or false?
2. How many table-wine appellations are there in Alsace?
3. If someone offers you a glass of Edelzwicker, what should you expect?
   a) one of the finest wines of Alsace, made from the Edelzwicker grape
   b) a blended white wine, usually of two different grape varietals
   c) a white wine made from the Pinot Noir grape, which is the only red variety allowed in Alsace
   d) a sparkling white wine made from any one of the white varieties grown in Alsace
4. Which of the following grape varieties would you *not* expect to find in a wine from Alsace?
   a) Riesling
   b) Gewürztraminer
   c) Chenin Blanc
   d) Pinot Blanc
   e) Sylvaner
   f) Muscat
   g) Pinot Gris
5. The term *gourmet* has a special meaning in Alsace; what does it represent?
6. Which vineyard does not belong in the following group?
   a) Les Murailles
   b) Les Sorcieres
   c) Les Maquisards
   d) Les Pucelles
   e) Les Amandiers

ANSWERS

1. *False. Although 95 percent of Alsace's production is white wine, a Rosé d'Alsace and a Rouge d'Alsace are also produced. They are both made from the Pinot Noir grape, which is the only red-wine variety allowed to be planted in the area. The Rouge is a light, dry, fruity wine, at its best when served slightly chilled.*

2. *Although the wine-producing area of Alsace is divided into two distinct regions, the Bas Rhin in the north and the Haut Rhin in the south, there is only one appellation, A.O.C. Alsace. Generally speaking, the best vineyards are located in the Haut Rhin. In order to distinguish which region a specific wine comes from, one looks for the address of the shipper, which must be printed on the label. When the actual name of the area is not mentioned, wines produced in the Bas Rhin may use the postal code 67, followed by three digits; those produced in the Haut Rhin use the postal code 68 followed by three digits.*

3. *b. Edelzwicker is a blended white wine.*

4. *c. Chenin Blanc is one of the primary grapes planted in the Loire Valley. Pinot Gris, by the way, is another name for Tokay d'Alsace.*

5. *In the Middle Ages, a gourmet was a special wine taster entitled to buy and sell the wines of Riquewihr, Alsace. Modern wine brokers in Alsace are still called gourmets.*

6. *d. Les Pucelles is a Premier Cru in Burgundy's Côte de Beaune. The remaining vineyards are all part of the Domaines du Château de Riquewihr, owned by the well-known firm of Dopff & Irion, Haut Rhin.*

The Loire

"Charming"

The Marquis de Lur-Saluces thus expressed his opinion of Muscadet.

1. Loire wines are generally named for the districts in which they are grown. True or false?

2. Which of the following wines are produced in the Loire Valley?

a) Cabernet d'Anjou
b) Pouilly-Fuissé
c) Quincy
d) Pouilly Fumé
e) Rosé d'Arbois
f) Quarts de Chaume

3. Bourgueil, Chinon, and Vouvray are subdistricts of:

a) Anjou
b) Quincy
c) Reuilly
d) Touraine

4. Match the wines with their principal grape varieties:

1. Pouilly-sur-Loire	a) Groslot
2. Rosé d'Anjou	b) Sauvignon Blanc
3. Chinon	c) Chenin Blanc
4. Vouvray	d) Cabernet Franc
5. Gros Plant du Pays Nantais	e) Folle Blanche
6. Sancerre	f) Chasselas

5. Match the following grape varieties with the names they are known by in the Loire:

1. Malbec	a) Pineau de la Loire
2. Cabernet Franc	b) Melon

3. Sauvignon Blanc — c) Cot
4. Muscadet — d) Blanc Fumé
5. Chenin Blanc — e) Breton

6. What red wine of the Loire has its own appellation?

7. If you prefer a dry wine, you should order a Rosé de la Loire rather than a Rosé d'Anjou. True or false?

8. Which subdistrict of Anjou is famous for its sweet white wines?

9. If it's a Bourgueil, it's got to be a red from Touraine. True or false?

10. Of the three Muscadet appellations, which is considered to be a) the finest? b) the largest?
1) Muscadet de Sèvre-et-Maine
2) Muscadet
3) Muscadet des Côteaux de la Loire

11. Name the VDQS *(Vin Délimité de Qualité Supérieure)* white wine produced in Nantes.

12. What does the term *sur lie* mean?

13. What was the first Appellation d'Origine of the Loire?

ANSWERS

1. *True. Muscadet, however, is an exception. Both the wine and the Muscadet appellation take their name from the grape variety.*

2. *a, c, d, f. Pouilly-Fuissé is a Burgundy; Rosé d'Arbois is produced in the Jura.*

3. *d. Touraine.*

4. *1–f, 2–a, 3–d, 4–c, 5–e, 6–b.*

5. *1–c, 2–e, 3–d, 4–b, 5–a.*

6. *Saumur-Champigny, a fruity red wine with a fragrant bouquet, is usually made from Cabernet Franc. Some producers may use Gamay, in which case Gamay will be indicated on the label.*

7. *True. Rosé de la Loire, a soft pink wine, is vinified dry. It must contain a minimum of 30 percent Cabernet, and it can be produced in Touraine as well as in Anjou-Saumur. Rosé d'Anjou, made from Groslot and Gamay, is usually slightly sweet and is often bottled in clear glass to display its light pink color.*

8. *The Côteaux du Layon produces sweet, and in some years very sweet, white wines that are absolutely glorious. The most famous vineyards are Bonnezeaux, with about 250 acres, and Quarts de Chaume, with approximately 125 acres. Both have their own Appellation Contrôlées. The wines are produced from Chenin Blanc.*

9. *True. The appellation Bourgueil is restricted to red and rosé wines. White wines produced in the area can only be called Touraine.*

10. *a) 1. Muscadet de Sèvre-et-Maine is considered to be the finest. Muscadet des Côteaux de la Loire is of medium quality, while simple Muscadet produces the lowest priced wines.*

b) 1. Muscadet de Sèvre-et-Maine is also the largest in area, with some 19,760 acres.

11. *Gros Plant du Pays Nantais is the VDQS wine.*

12. Sur lie, *literally "on its lees" (sediment), is a traditional technique in the Nantes region and applies to Muscadet as well as Gros Plant. In order for this designation to appear on a label, the wine must not have spent more than one winter in the barrels in which it was fermented and must still be on its lees when bottled; no racking is permitted. Wines produced by this technique sometimes have a refreshing* pétillant *quality (faint sparkle) and a fuller flavor.*

13. *Ménétou-Salon was the first, by decree in 1959.*

FLIGHT IV

Italy
Germany
Austria
Portugal
Spain
Hungary

Italy

The mythique about wine is half the fun.
The other two-thirds is the taste
And the remaining three fourths comes
From adequate imbibition.

Forbes Magazine
Editorial, July 15, 1974

1. Which of the following statements is incorrect?
   a) Italy is the largest wine producer in the world.
   b) Italy is the largest wine consumer in the world.
   c) Italy produces more types and varieties of wines than any other wine-producing nation in the world.
   d) Italy exports more wine to the United States than does any other country in the world.
   e) Two-thirds of the total Italian wine production is devoted to white varieties.

2. A map of the world shows that northern and central Italy are in the same latitude as:
   a) Canada and New England
   b) Maryland and Virginia
   c) Florida
   d) Cuba

3. Piedmont, Lombardy, Veneto, and Emilia-Romagna are wine regions located in:
   a) northern Italy
   b) central Italy
   c) southern Italy
   d) Sicily

4. Frascati is produced in:
a) northern Italy
b) central Italy
c) southern Italy
d) Sicily

5. Of the areas listed in Question 4, where is Corvo produced?

6. Pinot Grigio is a name for:
a) a town
b) an estate
c) a vineyard
d) a grape variety

7. Match the following wines with the regions in which they are produced.

1. Chianti	a) Emilia-Romagna
2. Soave	b) Piedmont
3. Orvieto	c) Tuscany
4. Verdicchio	d) Umbria
5. Lacrima Christi	e) Veneto
6. Lambrusco	f) Marches
7. Barolo	g) Campania

8. Which of the following is the most famous wine of Basilicata?
a) Aglianico del Vulture
b) Vino Nobile di Montepulciano
c) Brunello di Montalcino

9. Indicate whether the following wines are red (R) or white (W).

1. Amarone
2. Lambrusco
3. Bianco di Custoza
4. Sassella
5. Est! Est!! Est!!!
6. Dolcetto
7. Galestro
8. Vino Nobile di Montepulciano
9. Greco di Tufo
10. Cortese di Gavi
11. Vernaccia di Oristano

12. Brunello di Montalcino
13. Pinot Grigio
14. Frascati
15. Taurasi

10. Which one of the following grape varieties is considered to be the noble grape of northern Italy?
  a) Sangiovese
  b) Barbera
  c) Nebbiolo
  d) Cabernet Sauvignon

11. Which one of the grape varieties in Question 11 is the most widely planted quality red-wine variety in Italy?

12. Which one of the following white-grape varieties dominates in the production of Soave?
  a) Trebbiano
  b) Garganega
  c) Pinot Grigio
  d) Chardonnay

13. Of the two reds Valpolicella and Bardolino, both produced in the region of the Veneto, which is usually the firmer, fuller wine?

14. A Veronese specialty is Recioto, made from the *recie* (ears) of grape clusters. Before being pressed and fermented, the ripe ears are dried, somewhat like raisins, to concentrate their sugars. Slightly sweet Recioto della Valpolicella and sweet, sometimes sparkling, Recioto di Soave are made from dried red and white grapes respectively. Dry Recioto, called Amarone, is produced when all the sugar in the must is converted to alcohol during fermentation. The beauty of Reciotos lies in their rich, velvety character.
Now, the question is . . . what part of the grape bunch do the *ears* come from?
  a) only the outer grapes, excluding those within the bunch near the main stalk
  b) the top portion of the bunch, excluding the bottom
  c) the bottom portion of the bunch, excluding the top
  d) this is a joke; the entire bunch is used

15. What are the wine laws of Italy called?

16. All the best wines of Italy are designated as DOC. True or false?

17. What does DOCG refer to?

18. What was the first Italian wine to be granted the DOC designation?

19. Which was the first wine to be granted a DOCG rating?

20. Match the following words, found on Italian wine labels, with their correct definitions.

1. abboccato	a) white
2. amabile	b) cooperative cellars
3. bianco	c) sweet
4. brut	d) rosé
5. cantina sociale	e) slightly sweet
6. casa vinicola	f) red
7. classico	g) from the oldest part of the production area
8. consorzio	h) deep red (black)
9. dolce	i) farm
10. fattoria	j) dry
11. frizzante	k) estate
12. nero	l) harvest
13. rosato	m) sweeter than abboccato
14. rosso	n) a higher percentage of alcohol than the minimum required for that wine in general
15. secco	o) dry Spumante
16. superiore	p) old
17. tenuta	q) slightly sparkling
18. vecchio	r) winemakers' association
19. vendemmia	s) winery

21. What is the difference between Vino Tipico and Vino da Tavola?

22. In which year was Italy's DOC wine law passed by parliamentary legislation?
    a) 1492
    b) 1855
    c) 1963
    d) 1980

23. What name is given to the straw-covered flask of Chianti?

24. Traditionally, Chianti is a blend of both red and white grapes. True or false?

25. Is there such a wine as white Chianti?

26. Procanico, a white-grape variety, is another name for:
    a) Trebbiano Toscano
    b) Malvasia del Chianti
    c) Canaiolo, white
    d) Vernaccia

27. Just as Bordeaux in France is divided into various districts, so too the Chianti area of Italy is made up of zones. How many?

28. The seal of the Chianti Classico Consorzio found on the neck label of wines produced by its members depicts a:
    a) cherub with a grapevine
    b) coat of arms
    c) olive branch
    d) black rooster

29. The Riservas of the Classico zone are the longest-lived and most aristocratic of the Chianti region. True or false?

30. Which zones are covered by the Chianti Putto Consorzio?

31. If you were to find a bottle of red Italian wine labeled Tignanello, you would know that it was *not:*
    a) an estate-bottled wine
    b) produced in the Chianti Classico zone
    c) a DOC wine

d) produced by the Tuscan firm of Antinori
e) a wine with superb depth of flavor, ideal for aging

32. A special method of refermentation is sometimes used to add zest and roundness to certain Italian wines. The process involves picking a small quantity of grapes before the main harvest and drying them to concentrate the sugar. When the normal harvest is gathered and fermented, the dried grapes are added to the vats, inducing a secondary fermentation that helps to deepen the color and increase the alcohol, flavor, and vitality of the wine. What is this method called?

33. Podere Tre Torri di Traversagna, Cantina del Camino, Campi Raudii, Cinque Castelli, and Castello di Montalbano are all:
a) producers of Spanna
b) designations for Spannas produced by Vallana
c) red wines made from the Sangiovese grape
d) producers of Gattinara

34. If you were to find a bottle of Italian red wine labeled Brusco dei Barbi, you would know that it was *not:*
a) produced in Piedmont
b) produced by the *governo* method
c) big, bold, and elegant; ideal for aging
d) made at the Fattoria dei Barbi from Brunello (Sangiovese Grosso) grapes

35. Which Italian wine region has more DOC zones than any other?

36. The special bottle used by producers of premium red wines in the Langhe hills of central Piedmont is called a:
a) porcini
b) albeisa
c) torcolo
d) passito

37. What wine is called the king of Italian wines?

38. If you were to find a bottle of wine labeled Barolo, Riserva Speciale, you would expect it to be:
a) a full-bodied, high-alcohol red wine with a robust, violet, and tarlike bouquet, ideal for aging
b) made entirely from Michet, Lampia, or Rose subvarieties of the Nebbiolo grape
c) aged at least five years
d) all of the above
e) none of the above

39. The Nebbiolo grape derives its name from the Italian word *nebbia,* which means:
a) ink b) blue c) mist d) black pearl

40. Which wine does not belong in the following list:
a) Barolo
b) Gattinara
c) Barbaresco
d) Ghemme
e) Dolcetto
f) Boca
g) Lessona
h) Bramaterra

41. What is Sfursat, or Sforzato?
a) a robust red wine made from dried grapes grown in Valtellina, Lombardy
b) a soft, fruity red wine made entirely from Sangiovese grapes grown in Tuscany
c) a dry, light white wine produced from Teroldego grapes in Trentino-Alto Adige
d) a full-bodied and slightly tannic white wine made from Verduzzo grapes in Friuli-Venezia Giulia

42. If you were sipping a local wine in Luciano Pavarotti's hometown, what would your glass most likely contain?
a) Taurasi, a red wine named after the small town not far from Naples, in Campania
b) Regaleali Rosso del Conte, produced near Caltanissetta, Sicily
c) Lambrusco di Sorbara, produced near Modena, Emilia-Romagna

d) Sella & Mosca Torbato Secco di Alghero, produced at Alghero in Sardinia

43. Rubesco is the trademark name for what DOC wine?

44. What Italian grape variety is believed to be a relative of the Zinfandel grape of California?

45. The letter Q, stamped on a bottle of wine, is a regional mark of approval selectively bestowed by the Istituto Regionale della Vite e del Vino. Which region uses this mark of quality to distinguish its best wines?

46. Sicily is in the same latitude as:
a) Virginia
b) Florida
c) Cuba
d) Venezuela

47. What was the first DOC zone of Sicily?

48. Julius Caesar served a wine from Sicily to celebrate his third election as Consul of Rome. The same wine is still produced in limited quantities. What is it called?
a) Pachino
b) Mamertino
c) Moscato di Pantelleria
d) Rapitalà

49. Which one of the following grape varieties would you *not* expect to find in a white wine from Sicily:
a) Cataratto
b) Inzolia
c) Pinot Grigio
d) Grillo

50. Match the following Italian wine regions with the numbered regions on the map.
a) Abruzzo
b) Apulia
c) Basilicata
d) Calabria
e) Campania
f) Emilia Romagna

g) Friuli-Venezia Giulia
h) Latium
i) Liguria
j) Lombardy
k) Marches
l) Molise
m) Piedmont
n) Sardinia
o) Sicily
p) Trentino-Alto Adige
q) Tuscany
r) Umbria
s) Valle d'Aosta
t) Veneto

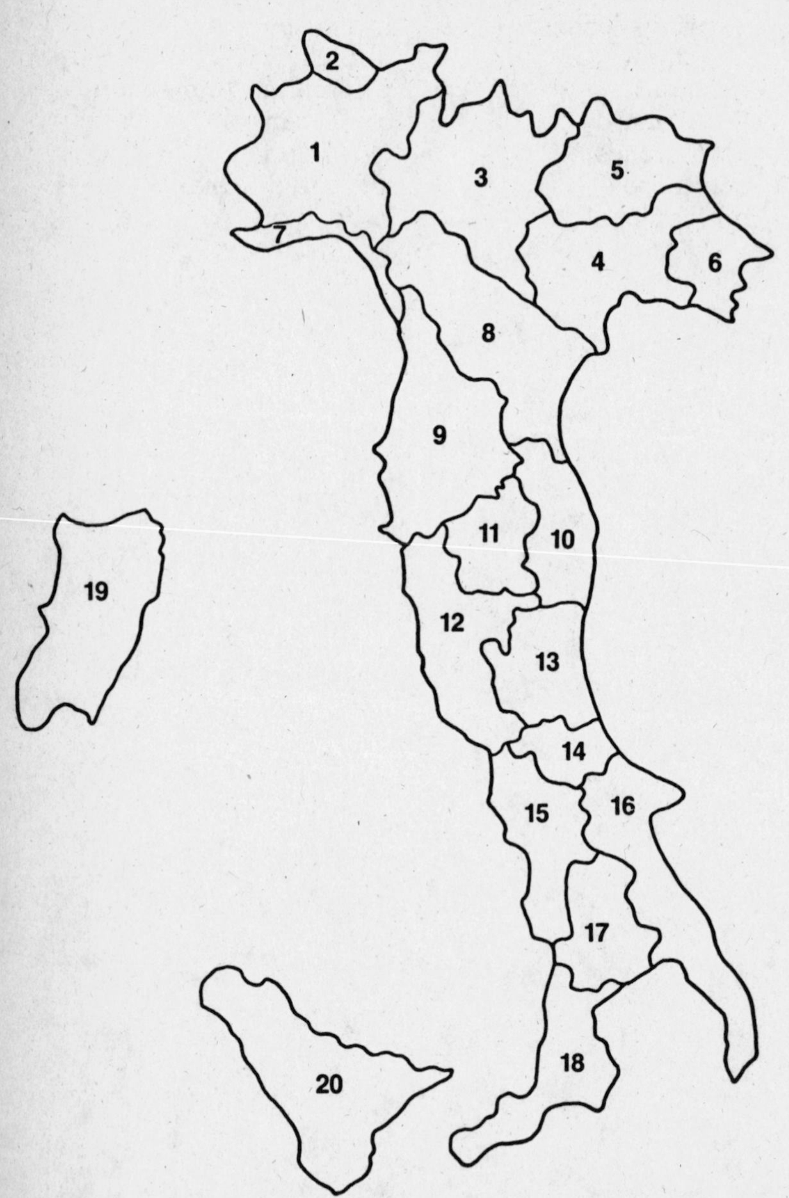

2
1
3
5
7
4
6
8
9
11
10
19
12
13
14
15
16
17
20
18

ANSWERS

1. *e. Two-thirds of the total Italian wine production is devoted to* red *varieties, not white.*

2. *a. Canada and New England.*

3. *a. northern Italy.*

4. *b. central Italy. Frascati is a white Roman wine, produced in the region of Latium.*

5. *d. Sicily.*

6. *d. Pinot Grigio is the name for a grape variety otherwise known as Pinot Gris.*

7. *1–c, 2–e, 3–d, 4–f, 5–g, 6–a, 7–b.*

8. *a. Aglianico del Vulture, a dry red wine, produced from Aglianico grapes grown on the slopes of the extinct volcano Vulture, can be one of the best wines of southern Italy. Vino Nobile di Montepulciano and Brunello di Montalcino are both red wines produced in Tuscany.*

9. *1–R, 2–R, 3–W, 4–R, 5–W, 6–R, 7–W, 8–R, 9–W, 10–W, 11–W, 12–R, 13–W, 14–W, 15–R.*

10. *c. Nebbiolo is considered the noble grape of northern Italy.*

11. *a. Sangiovese—also known as Sangiovese Grosso (Brunello), Sangioveto, Prugnolo, and Prugnolo Gentile—is the most widely planted quality red-wine grape in Italy. It is used to produce such red wines as Chianti, Brunello di Montalcino, and Torgiano Rosso.*

12. *b. Garganega makes up 70 to 90 percent of the Soave blend; Trebbiano di Soave is used in proportions of 10 to 30 percent.*

13. *Valpolicella is usually the firmer, fuller wine.*

14. *b. the top portion of the bunch, excluding the bottom. The lower part of each grape cluster is cut off before ripening, and only the upper part, or ears, which receive the most sun, is left to ripen.*

15. *Italy's wine laws go by the name* Denominazione di Origine Controllata, *or DOC for short. When a wine is labeled DOC, it is understood that both the wine's place of origin and its production methods are controlled by the Italian government. There are over two hundred DOC wine zones in Italy.*

16. *False. For various reasons, some excellent Italian wines are not classified as DOC. Spanna, produced in Piedmont, is just one example of a non-DOC wine with a superlative reputation.*

17. *DOCG indicates the highest level of the DOC laws. DOCG wines are not only controlled by the Italian government, but they are also guaranteed. The designation is granted only to DOC producers who voluntarily submit their wines to testing by the Ministry of Agriculture and Forestry. The wines must be bottled at the winery and have a tamper-proof state seal affixed to the top of each bottle by the state authorities. Wines submitted that do not meet the DOCG standards are declassified to the status of table wines, the lowest category designated by law, losing even their DOC status for that particular vintage.*

18. *In 1966 Vernaccia di San Gimignano, produced in Tuscany, became the first DOC wine.*

19. *In 1980 Brunello di Montalcino was the first to be approved as a DOCG wine. Barolo, Barbaresco, and Vino Nobile di Montepulciano followed soon after, and others will no doubt be added to this distinguished list in due course. The first DOCG wines will not appear on the market, however, until the mid-1980s, due to aging requirements for each wine.*

20. *1–e, 2–m, 3–a, 4–o, 5–b, 6–s, 7–g, 8–r, 9–c, 10–i, 11–q, 12–h, 13–d, 14–f, 15–j, 16–n, 17–k, 18–p, 19–l.*

21. *Vino Tipico refers to a wine whose area of production and grape variety are named on the label. This category is one step below DOC. Vino da Tavola (table wine), according to Common Market regulations, refers to all wines that are non-DOC or that do not fall within the new Vino Tipico category. This is a catchall term and does not in itself imply any particular level of quality.*

22. *c. 1963.*

23. *The straw-covered flask of Chianti is called a fiasco. Although its use is fast disappearing today, it is thought that the straw covering was originally devised by peasants to keep the wine cool while they worked under the hot sun. The fiasco was later used to protect the bulbous hand-blown bottles from breaking during transport.*

24. *True. Although there is a growing trend away from the use of white grapes in Chianti, the DOC requires some white grapes in the blend of any wine labeled as Chianti.*

25. *No, not since the DOC laws came into effect. Although white wines are made in the area, the Chianti designation is restricted only to the production of red wines.*

26. *a. Trebbiano Toscano.*

27. *There are seven zones in Chianti: Rufina (the smallest), Montalbano, Colline Pisane, Colli Senesi (the largest), Colli Fiorentini, Colli Aretini, and Classico (the heart of Chianti).*

28. *d. a black rooster, known in Italy as the gallo nero.*

29. *True. With few exceptions, Chianti Classico Riservas are fuller in body, more tannic, and require more aging than the other wines of Chianti.*

30. *The Chianti Putto Consorzio protects and promotes the wines produced from the six Chianti zones, outside the Classico zone.*

31. *c. Tignanello is not a DOC wine, even though it's produced in the Classico zone. The reason for this is that Antonori produced the wine as an example of what could be achieved if the required white grapes were omitted from the usual Chianti formula. In place of the white grapes Trebbiano and Malvasia, Tignanello contains a small percentage of Cabernet Sauvignon, which gives the wine a better structure. Originally produced as an experiment, this extraordinary wine was received with such fervor that it is now produced as one of Antonori's most prestigious efforts, in limited quantities and only in exceptional vintages.*

32. *The method is called governo. Although its use is not restricted to one area, it is most often used in Tuscany.*

33. *b. designations for Spannas produced by Vallana, one of the most distinguished firms in the area, if not* the *most distinguished.*

34. *a. Brusco dei Barbi, a relatively unknown delight, is produced at Montalcino in Tuscany, not in Piedmont.*

35. *Piedmont has the most, with thirty-six DOC zones.*

36. *b. albeisa. The distinctive bottle is Bordeaux in style, but with more sloping shoulders. Its design was inspired by the bottles used in the Langhe during Napoleon's era.*

37. *Barolo is called the king of Italian wines. In fact, it is also the wine of kings, or at least one king, anyway. Italy's first king, Victor Emmanuel II, liked Barolo so much that he established his own vineyards and winery, Fontana Fredda, at Serralunga d'Alba in Piedmont.*

38. *d. all of the above.*

39. *c. mist. The grape is so named because a mist shrouds the Nebbiolo vineyards at harvest time.*

40. *e. Dolcetto is a red wine made from the Dolcetto grape in Piedmont. The others are also red wines produced in the Piedmont region, but they are made entirely or mainly from the Nebbiolo grape.*

41. *a. a robust red wine made from dried grapes grown in Valtellina, Lombardy.*

42. *c. Lambrusco di Sorbara. Pavarotti was born in Modena, the heart of Lambrusco production in the region of Emilia-Romagna.*

43. *Torgiano Rosso, produced in Umbria, is better known by Lungarotti's trademark name Rubesco.*

44. *The Primitivo, grown primarily in Apulia, is thought to be a relative of California's Zinfandel.*

45. *Since 1966, Sicily has stamped its best wines with the letter Q (Marchio di Qualitá, or Mark of Quality). The words* Regione Siciliana *appear within the center of the Q.*

46. *a. Virginia.*

47. *In 1968 Etna became the first DOC zone of Sicily.*

48. *b. Mamertino is produced in the province of Messina from white grapes, primarily Cataratto, blended with Inzolia and Grillo. It's more of a dessert wine than a table wine.*

49. *c. Pinot Grigio is grown in the cooler areas of northern Italy, primarily in Tre Venezie or Triveneto, the area encompassing the three regions Trentino-Alto Adige, Veneto, and Friuli-Venezia Giulia.*

50. *a–13, b–16, c–17, d–18, e–15, f–8, g–6, h–12, i–7, j–3, k–10, l–14, m–1, n–19, o–20, p–5, q–9, r–11, s–2, t–4.*

Germany

1. Germany is the northern most winegrowing country in the world. True or false?
2. Germany produces more white wine than red. True or false?
3. May wine is a light Rhine wine that has been sweetened and flavored with a particular herb. What is the name of the herb?
4. What color bottle is used for:
   a) Rhine wines?
   b) Mosel wines?
5. One can immediately recognize a wine from Franken (Franconia) by the distinctive shape of the bottle. What is this famous bottle called?
6. Which of the following grape varieties would *not* be found in a wine from Germany?
   a) Silvaner
   b) Chardonnay
   c) Riesling
   d) Müller-Thurgau
7. Which of the grape varieties in Question 6 is considered to be the finest grape of Germany?
8. Of the varieties listed in Question 6, which is the most widely planted wine grape in Germany?
9. The Müller-Thurgau vine is thought to be the result of a cross between:
   a) Riesling and Scheurebe
   b) Riesling and Kerner

c) Riseling and Rülander
d) Riesling and Silvaner

10. If you had a Rülander vine growing in your yard, a French winegrower would identify it as:
a) Pinot Gris
b) Pinot Blanc
c) Muscadet
d) Chenin Blanc

11. The normal harvest in Germany takes place sooner than the normal harvest in France. True or false?

12. Zeller Schwarze Katz, Bereich Bernkastel, Moselblümchen, and Piesporter Michelsberg are examples of:
a) regional wines from the Rhine
b) the finest wines of the Rhine
c) regional wines from the Mosel
d) the finest wines of the Mosel

13. Blue Nun is:
a) a regional wine from the Rhine
b) a Liebfraumilch
c) a trademark name for a blended white wine from Germany
d) a Qualitätswein b.A.
e) all of the above

14. Ahr, Mosel-Saar-Ruwer, Mittelrhein, Rheingau, Nahe, Rheinhessen, Rheinpfalz, Hessische Bergstrasse, Franconia, Württemberg, and Baden are the names of the eleven designated quality wine regions of Germany. Which is:
a) the largest wine-producing region?
b) the smallest region?

15. The wines produced in the region called Mosel-Saar-Ruwer are earthy, heavy, and long-lived. True or false?

16. What special soil element, present in the vineyards of the middle Mosel, helps the grapes to grow in this cold climate?

17. Of the eleven wine regions listed in Question 14, which are the only two that have not been subdivided into two or more districts, called bereich?

18. Of the eleven wine regions, which two are noted for their production of red wines?

19. Of the eleven wine regions, which is the most northern and which is the most southern?

20. Where does Liebfraumilch come from?
a) the Rheinhessen
b) the Rheinpfalz
c) the Nahe
d) any of the above
e) anywhere in Germany

21. Where is Steinwein produced?

22. What is the British term for Rhine wine?

23. Prior to the German wine law of 1971, there were more than twenty thousand individual vineyard names registered in Germany. The new law decreed that no single vineyard should be less than 12.5 acres in size, and it allowed for the grouping of several vineyards with similar characteristics into general sites.
a) What are these collective vineyard sites called?
b) What are the remaining individual sites called?

24. Of the four categories of German wines, which is the finest?
a) Qualitätswein bestimmter Anbaugebiete (Q.b.A.)
b) Qualitätswein mit Prädikat
c) Deutscher Landwein
d) Deutscher Tafelwein

25. Gallization (chaptalisation), the addition of sugar to grape must in order to increase the resulting alcohol content in a wine, is *not* permitted in which of the categories listed in Question 24?

26. In the category name Qualitätswein bestimmter Anbaugebiete, what does the word *Anbaugebiete* refer to?
    a) Germany's eleven wine regions
    b) the districts (bereich) within the eleven regions
    c) the collective vineyard sites
    d) individual vineyard sites

27. Which of the categories in Question 24 was created in 1982 and is essentially equivalent to the French Vin de Pays appellation?

28. The *Öchsle* scale is used to measure:
    a) the alcohol content of a wine
    b) the sugar density of the grape must (unfermented juice)
    c) the acidity of the grapes
    d) the acidity of the wine

29. There are six wines legally designated as having special attributes, or *Prädikat.* They are listed below in alphabetical order; number them in order of ascending sweetness, with (#1) as the driest:
    Auslese
    Beerenauslese
    Eiswein
    Kabinett
    Spätlese
    Trockenbeerenauslese

30. A guest asks for a dry German wine. In your refrigerator you have a bottle of Liebfraumilch and a bottle of Kabinett. Which wine do you serve?

31. The specific *Prädikat* designations listed in Question 29 are determined by:
    a) the sugar content of the must
    b) the time when the grapes are harvested

c) the honesty of each grower
d) the yield of grapes per acre

32. The term *Auslese* on a wine label indicates that the wine was made from:
a) grapes picked later than usual
b) individually selected bunches of grapes, from which all unripe berries have been discarded
c) grapes that have been picked one at a time from selected bunches
d) shriveled, overripe grapes that have been picked one at a time

33. Using the definitions in Question 32, Trockenbeerenauslese, (TBA for short) indicates that a wine was made from a, b, c, or d?

34. The full range of Prädikat wines are produced every year. True or false?

35. Eiswein (ice wine) is made from fully ripened grapes that were caught by a sudden sharp frost during harvest. The frozen grapes are picked and quickly pressed before they have a chance to thaw. The resulting wine is sweeter and richer than it would have been had the grapes been picked before the frost. True or false?

36. As of 1982, Eiswein can be made from:
a) frozen Kabinett grapes
b) frozen Spätlese grapes
c) frozen Auslese grapes
d) frozen Beerenauslese grapes
e) frozen Trockenbeerenauslese grapes
f) all of the above
g) only c, d, and e

37. What formula is used to convert degrees *Öchsle* to degrees *Brix*, the scale used in the United States for measuring the sugar content of grapes and must?

38. Spätlese, Auslese, and Beerenauslese wines must be made from grapes infected with the *Botrytis cinerea* mold. True or false?

39. What is the German word for *Botrytis cinerea?*

40. Match the following words found on German wine labels with their correct definitions.

1. abfüller
2. abgefüllt durch
3. abgefüllt für
4. erzeugerabfüllung
5. halbtrocken
6. lieblich
7. rot
8. süss
9. trocken
10. weingut
11. weiss
12. weissherbst
13. winzer
14. winzergenossenschaft
15. winzerverein

a) semisweet
b) estate-bottled
c) dry
d) bottler
e) red
f) white
g) bottled for
h) bottled by
i) cooperative association of grape growers that have set up a winery and cellar
j) cooperative of smaller growers
k) semidry
l) sweet
m) grape grower
n) vineyard property
o) white wine from red grapes

41. Schloss Vollrads, Schloss Johannisberg, Steinberg, and Schloss Reichartschausen are four of the greatest vineyards, or lagen, in all of Germany. In which wine region are they located?

42. If you've read Frank Schoonmaker's classic, *The Wines of Germany,* revised by Peter Sichel, you would know that *Bingen pencil* is a colloquial German term for:

a) the device for measuring the sugar content of ripe grapes
b) a wooden stake used to support Rhine vines

c) Rhine wine with a splash of Cassis
d) a corkscrew

43. If you wanted to visit the outstanding wine estates of von Buhl, Bürcklin-Wolf, and Bassermann-Jordan, known collectively as "the three B's," which region would you set out for?

44. Who is regarded as the father of German viticulture?

ANSWERS

1. *True.*

2. *True. Only* 12 percent *of Germany's production is red wine.*

3. *May wine is flavored with woodruff (*waldmeister *in German).*

4. *a. brown.*
b. green.

5. *The Franken bottle, shaped like a squat flagon, is known as a* bocksbeutel. *It is so named because to the Franconians it resembles a goat's scrotum,* bock *meaning "goat,"* beutel *meaning "bag."*

6. *b. Chardonnay. The other three are the most prevalent varieties in Germany.*

7. *c. Riesling is considered the king of German grape varieties, and wines produced from the Riesling are the finest of Germany. It accounts for about 23 percent of the white-grape varieties cultivated in the country.*

8. *d. Müller-Thurgau is the most widely planted grape variety in Germany, with some 61,775 acres under cultivation.*

9. *d. Riesling and Silvaner.*

10. *Pinot Gris is the French name for the Rülander.*

11. *False. The German harvest rarely begins before mid-October, and in exceptional years it may last through November.*

12. *c. regional wines from the Mosel.*

13. *e. all of the above.*

14. *a) the Rheinpfalz, also known as the Palatinate, is the largest.*
b) Hessische Bergstrasse is the smallest region.

15. *False. Wines from the Mosel-Saar-Ruwer are usually light and fruity, with a captivating flowery perfume. Only the best wines, produced in exceptional years, can be stored for any length of time.*

16. *A deposit of slate, often the size of roof shingles, covers the topsoil of the middle Mosel vineyards. Slate absorbs and stores up the sun's warmth during the day and releases it at night.*

17. *The Ahr and the Rheingau both have only one bereich; the bereich for the Ahr is Walporzheim/Ährtal and the bereich for the Rheingau is Johannisberg.*

18. *The Ahr and Württemberg are noted for their red wines.*

19. *The Ahr is the northernmost wine region; Baden is the southernmost.*

20. *d. As of April 1982, Liebfraumilch can only be produced in the Rheinhessen, the Rheinpfalz, or in the Nahe; the region of production must be stated on the label. Prior to this date, German vintners were allowed to blend Liebfraumilch from wines produced in four regions: the Rheingau and the three mentioned above.*

21. *True Steinwein is produced at the Stein, Germany's largest single vineyard site (275 acres), located at Würzburg, Franconia. The term Steinwein is often loosely applied to all wines produced in Franconia.*

22. *Hock is the British term for Rhine wine; its name is derived from the village of Hochheim in the Rheingau.*

23. *a) Collective vineyard sites are called* grosslagen; *there are approximately 130 of these in Germany.*

b) Individual vineyard sites are called einzellagen, or lagen *for short. There are approximately 2,600 lagen in Germany today.*

24. *b. Qualitätswein mit Prädikat is the finest category, translated as "quality wines with special attributes."*

25. *b. Qualitätswein mit Prädikat wines may never be chaptalised, according to the law. The other categories may be, if necessary, when the grapes do not ripen sufficiently.*

26. *a. Germany's eleven wine regions. Q.b.A. translates as "quality wines from specified growing regions."*

27. *c. Deutscher Landwein is the category created for wines produced in any one of fifteen newly designated regions within the German wine-growing area. Landwein ranks between Deutscher Tafelwein and Q.b.A. Following is a list of the fifteen newly designated Landwein regions:*

Ahetaler Landwein	*Starkenburger Landwein*
Rheinburgen Landwein	*Landwein der Mosel*
Nahegauer Landwein	*Landwein der Saar*
Altrheingauer Landwein	*Rheinischer Landwein*
Pfalzer Landwein	*Fränkischer Landwein*
Regensburger Landwein	*Bayerischer Bodensee Landwein*
Schwäbischer Landwein	*Unterbadischer Landwein*
Südbadischer Landwein	

28. *b. the sugar density of the grape must. The scale is named for Ferdinand Öchsle, the German physicist who devised it in the early nineteenth century.*

29. *1–Kabinett, 2–Spätlese, 3–Auslese, 4–Beerenauslese, 5–Eiswein, 6–Trockenbeerenauslese.*

30. *The Kabinett is drier.*

31. *a. Although the harvest time has something to do with the degree of ripeness in the grapes (the later they're harvested, the riper they should become), it is the measured sugar content of the must that ultimately dictates which designation a wine will bear.*

32. *b. individually selected bunches of grapes.*

33. *d.* Trocken *means "dry" and* beeren *means "berries," thus we have dried berries, or shriveled, overripe grapes.*

34. *False. Although Kabinett and Spätlese are frequently produced, in some years the grapes do not ripen sufficiently to make the sweetest wines in the Prädikat catagory. 1972 is an example of a poor vintage; no Prädikat wines were produced that year, not even in the Kabinett category.*

35. *True. Eiswein has an extraordinary concentration of both acidity and sweetness, since the frozen water portion of the grapes, in the shape of ice pellets, is removed during pressing and prior to fermentation.*

36. *d. A 1982 amendment to the German wine law of 1971 now restricts the production of Eiswein solely to frozen grapes of the Beerenauslese category. Thus, in Question 29, Eiswein takes its position between Beerenausleese and T.B.A. Previously, Eiswein could be made from frozen grapes in any of the five Prädikat categories.*

37. *To convert degrees* Öchsle *to degrees* Brix, *divide the degrees* Öchsle *by 4 and subtract 2.5.*

38. *False. While the best of these wines are made from rotted grapes,* botrytis *has never been a requirement of Spätlese, Auslese, or Beerenauslese wines. In addition, the German wine laws of 1971 also eliminated* botrytis *as a requirement for Trockenbeerenauslese. In some years, late harvested grapes lose water even without* botrytis *so that the juice is still concentrated enough to make a rich, sweet wine.*

39. Edelfäule *is the German word for* Botrytis cinerea.

40. *1-d, 2-h, 3-g, 4-b, 5-k, 6-a, 7-e, 8-l, 9-c, 10-n, 11-f, 12-o, 13-m, 14-i, 15-j.*

41. *These great wine estates are located in the Rheingau.*

42. *d. Frank Schoonmaker tells us, "The term* Bingen pencils *originated during a city council meeting in Bingen. The mayor asked one of the city councilors for a pencil, and it turned out that none of the city councilors had pencils, but they all had corkscrews. Hence the origin of the word* Bingen pencil."

43. *The three B's can be found in the Rheinpfalz, more specifically in the bereich of Middle Haardt, where the best Palatinate wines are produced.*

44. *The Roman Emperor Probus, who reigned from 276 until 282, is regarded as the father of German viticulture. It seems that shortly after Caesar's conquest of Gaul, a law was passed that forbade the planting of grape vines in the Roman colonies. Probus, who is also called the Wine Emperor, revoked this law in the third century and thus is remembered as the father of German viticulture, even though it's doubtful that he ever tasted a German wine.*

Austria

1. Most Austrian vines are trained to grow on trellises several feet above the ground so that the leaves can get maximum sunlight. Who developed this technique, known as the high culture method?

2. Which major Austrian wine region is divided into eight subregions?
   a) Styria
   b) Lower Austria
   c) Burgenland
   d) Vienna

3. In which wine region is the Rust-Lake Neusiedl area located?

4. What is *schluck?*

5. What is the most widely planted white-wine grape in Austria?

6. Which grape variety does not belong in the following group:
   a) Blaufraenkisch (Gamay)
   b) Blau Portugieser
   c) Weisser Burgunder
   d) St. Laurent
   e) Blauer Burgunder

7. Rotgipfler and Zierfandler (also called Spätrot) are two grape varieties used in a blended white wine that is unique to one Austrian wine region. Name the region.

8. What is the name of the light red (rosé) wine produced as a specialty in West Styria?

9. The must weight (sugar content) of unfermented grape

juice in Austria is measured by the Klosterneuburg Mostwaage (KMW) scale, which was developed at the Klosterneuburg Abbey in 1876. Who developed it?

10. Ausbruch, a quality classification traditionally found on the labels of certain sweet wines produced in the Burgenland region, was legally defined by the Austrian wine law of 1961. The Ausbruch designation may only be used for wines whose quality is between:
a) Qualitätswein and Kabinett
b) Kabinett and Spätlese
c) Spätlese and Auslese
d) Auslese and Beerenauslese
e) Beerenauslese and Trockenbeerenauslese

11. In Austria, red wines are sometimes produced as Spätlese. True or false?

12. More red wine is produced in Austria than white wine. True or false?

13. What Austrian term has a double meaning, designating the new wine of the previous harvest and also applying to the wine taverns where such wine is served by the glass or in carafes?

ANSWERS

1. *The high culture technique was developed by the late Prof. Dr. Lenz Moser (Lenz Moser III). The system has now been accepted internationally, and vineyards all over the world are using this method.*

2. *b. Lower Austria; the wine subregions are Falkenstein, Retz, Wachau, Krems, Langenlois, Klosterneuburg, Gumpoldskirchen, and Voeslau.*

3. *The Rust-Lake Neusiedl area is located in the Burgenland region. Over 90 percent of all Burgenland wines are produced in this area.*

4. *Schluck is the local name for the ordinary white wine produced in the region of Wachau. It's a delightful quaffing wine when drunk young.*

5. *The Grüner Veltliner is the most widely planted white-wine grape in Austria. It produces a varietal-labeled dry wine that is short-lived, but wonderfully spicy, fruity, and lively.*

6. *c. Weisser Burgunder (Pinot Blanc) is a white-grape variety; the others are red varieties.*

7. *Gumpoldskirchen, located in Lower Austria, is the home of the popular blended wine made from Rotgipfler and Zierfandler grapes—the former contributing more to the wine's character and the latter more to its aroma. Another white variety, the Neuburger, may also be used in the blend.*

8. *Schilcher, made from the Blauer Wildbacher grape, which only grows in this area, is the unique light red (rosé) wine produced in West Styria.*

9. *In 1860 the first school of viticulture was established in Austria* *at the Klosterneuburg Abbey. Its director, Freiherr von Babo, developed the KMW wine scales, still in use today, to determine the sugar content of unfermented must. One degree KMW equals approximately five degrees on the Öechsle scale.*

10. *e. Beerenhauslese and Trockenbeerenauslese.*

11. *True. The Blauer Burgunder (Pinot Noir) is sometimes made as a Spätlese, fermented to dryness. Although high in alcohol in this style, the wine is smooth, with a delicate bouquet and good body.*

12. *False. About 90 percent of the wines produced in Austria are white.*

13. *Heurigen is a term describing both new wine and the tavern where it is served. During the reign of Joseph II in the eighteenth century, a dispensation was granted allowing growers to sell their own wine in their homes. This decree laid the legal foundation for the festive wine taverns called Heurigen, which are so much a convivial part of today's Austrian social scene. Those who sell Heurigen, or new wine, hang a pine bough or wreath outside their establishment to alert passersby that these refreshing wines are available.*

Portugal

1. Port, Madeira, and rosé are the only wines produced in Portugal. True or false?

2. The wine Mateus (pronounced Ma-*táy*-us) is named for a:
   a) swan
   b) palace
   c) vineyard
   d) grape variety

3. The charm of Vinhos Verdes depends on their freshness and youth. True or false?

4. Vinho Verde wines are so named because:
   a) the grapes are picked before they're ripe
   b) the wines have a distinctly green tinge
   c) the Minho province, where they're produced, is extremely green and fertile
   d) it's the only Portuguese wine sold in a tall, green bottle

5. Which soil element is characteristic of the vineyards in the Minho province?
   a) granite
   b) sand
   c) chalk
   d) clay

6. The vines in the Minho province are trained to grow unusually high to protect the buds from ground frosts in the spring and because the soil is so rich, that the vines would die if they were pruned. Which of the following terms is used to describe the way in which the vines are trained?
   a) enforcado (up trees)
   b) latada (on trellises)

c) cruzeta (on wooden crosses)
d) all of the above

7. The pétillant (slightly effervescent) quality of Vinho Verde comes from:
a) the high acid in the grapes
b) a special variety of grape
c) the addition of carbonic gas
d) a malolactic fermentation in the bottle

8. The wines of Bucelas are made primarily from the Arinto grape; what color are the wines?

9. The vineyards of Colares are unusual because:
a) they are fertilized with seagull droppings
b) spray from the Atlantic crusts the grapes with salt
c) the vines are planted in sand dunes
d) they are irrigated with salt water from the Atlantic

10. The vines of Colares were the first in Portugal to be ravaged by *phylloxera*, an infestation that destroyed most European vineyards in the nineteenth century. True or false?

11. Which grape variety is used to produce the red wines of Colares?
a) Ramisco
b) Periquita
c) Touriga
d) Bastardo

12. Which grape variety in Question 11 takes its name from the vineyard where it was first planted, and produces a flavorful, medium-bodied red wine of the same name?

13. No Portuguese wines are made with Cabernet Sauvignon. True or false?

14. A close approximation of the Portuguese pronunciation of Dão, a wine region in northern Portugal which produces excellent wines of the same name, would be:

a) dow
b) don
c) dang
d) day

15. What rare, red table wine is as much sought after in Portugal as is the legendary 'Vega Sicilia' in Spain?

16. What was the first wine region in the world to be officially demarcated (government-controlled)?

17. What restaurant in the United States is renowned for its collection of Portuguese wines, the most extensive list in America?

ANSWERS

1. *False. The country also produces quality dry red and white table wines.*

2. *b. palace.*

3. *True. Their lifespan is short and they should not be kept for any length of time.*

4. *c. The Minho province, where they're produced, is extremely green and fertile. Contrary to what some people believe, the grapes are never picked before they're ripe.*

5. *a. granite.*

6. *d. all of the above.*

7. *c, d. The best wines undergo a malolactic fermentation in the bottle; wines of lesser quality are injected with carbonic gas.*

8. *The Arinto grape is considered to be related to the Riesling of Germany; the wines are white.*

9. *c. The vines are planted in sand dunes. It should be noted, however, that the vines take root in a subsoil of clay beneath the sand. To plant them, workers must dig trenches, sometimes several meters deep, until the firm subsoil is reached where the vine shoots can get a good grip. The work is dangerous; a few men have lost their lives, or come close to it, by being buried in a cave-in. Today the workers wear baskets on their heads so that if they are buried they will have enough air space to breath until they are rescued.*

10. *False. Colares is one of the few areas in the world that escaped the ravages of* phylloxera. *The louse cannot survive in sand, so the vines of Colares were never infested.*

11. *a. Ramisco.*

12. *b. Periquita. In 1840, José María da Fonseca grafted an unknown red grape, Castelão, at his estate, Periquita, near his wine cellars at Azeitão. The wine produced from this grape was so unique that it became known as "the wine from Periquita." The name remains a registered trademark of J. M. da Fonseca.*

13. *False. Since 1976, a fine red wine called Camarete Clarete has been produced with a large percentage of Cabernet Sauvignon, grown as an experiment on the Arrábida Peninsula. One has to visit Portugal to drink it, however, since none is exported.*

14. *a. Dow. Try to make it nasal, hold your nose, if necessary, and you will say it just about right.*

15. *Barca Velha, rare because of its infrequent and limited production, is produced in the Douro by the Port firm of Ferreira. The dry, red table wine, a blend of three Port grapes, is only produced in certain years. The first vintage was 1951; others include '57, '64, '65, and '66. The best place to find it is at some of the better-known restaurants in Lisbon.*

16. *The Douro was the first, in 1756. Although it is famous for its Port wine, 60 percent of its output is table wine.*

17. La Terrasse, *a first class establishment in Philadelphia, has the most extensive Portuguese wine list in the United States. Pasquale Iocca, their wine and spirit director, is a Portuguese wine expert, and he should be able to answer any further questions you have on Portuguese wines.*

Spain

1. All Rioja is red. True or false?
2. Which of the following wines is not made in Rioja:
   a) Tinto
   b) Clarete
   c) Sherry
   d) Rosado
3. Rioja wines are usually a blend, made from several grape varieties. True or false.
4. Which of the following grape varieties should you *not* expect to find in a red wine from Rioja:
   a) Tempranillo
   b) Cabernet Sauvignon
   c) Garnacho
   d) Graciano
   e) Mazuelo
5. Of the varieties listed in Question 4, which is the dominant grape used in the red wines of Rioja?
6. Of Rioja's three subdistricts—Rioja Alta, Rioja Alavesa, and Rioja Baja—which is:
   a) the smallest zone?
   b) the largest zone?
   c) the zone located on the northeastern bank of the Rio Ebro?
7. Alta means "upper," Baja means "lower"; where does the word *Alavesa* come from?
   a) the Spanish word for middle
   b) a river

c) a province
d) a vineyard

8. From which of the choices listed in Question 7 does Rioja take its name?

9. The names seen on Rioja labels, such as Viña Tondonia, Viña Real, Viña Pomal, Monte Real, Banda Azul, and Brillante, are:
   a) generic (regional) names
   b) varietal names
   c) proprietary (brand) names
   d) vineyard names

10. French grape growers moved from Bordeaux into Rioja in the late 1800s because:
    a) they were forced from their land due to urban sprawl
    b) *Phylloxera* had devastated the French vineyards
    c) the French government increased land taxes
    d) a French wine glut had reduced the demand for grapes

11. In Rioja, what does the term *bordelesa* refer to?
    a) a claret-style red wine aged a maximum of two years in French oak
    b) a method of fermentation that involves a longer vatting period to extract the maximum color from the skins of the grapes
    c) a fifty-five-gallon barrel made of French oak
    d) an eighty-four-gallon barrel made of American oak

12. If you invited a man from La Mancha to dinner, which of the following wines would make him feel right at home?
    a) Rioja
    b) Sherry
    c) Valdepeñas
    d) Extrísimo

13. Where is Extrísimo produced, and how did it come by its unusual name?

14. Match the following bodegas (winemaking concerns) with the area in which they're located.

1. Federico Paternina	a) Penedès
2. Jean Leon	b) Rioja
3. Olarra	c) Valbuena de Duero (Valladolid)
4. Torres	
5. Vega Sicilia	

15. If you were to ask the proprietor of a Spanish bodega to let you see his *bodeguero,* who or what would you expect to encounter?

a) a wooden wine press
b) a vaulted storage cellar
c) the winemaker
d) the cat who keeps away the mice

16. There are basically two types of red wine produced in Spain, clarete and tinto. Which description generally fits which type?

a) a light red wine
b) a full-flavored, deep ruby wine

17. Of the three growing districts in Penedès, the Baix Penedès, Penedès Medio, and Alt Penedès, which is:

a) better suited to growing red grapes?
b) particularly suited to growing white grapes?

18. The red-grape variety called Tempranillo in Rioja is known as Ull de Llebra in Penedès, where Catalan is the traditional language. What is the literal translation of Ull de Llebra?

a) nose of the turtle
b) eye of the hare
c) blush of the maiden
d) blood of the bull

19. Which of these grape varieties are used to make white wine in Penedès?

a) Parellada

b) Macabeo (Viura)
c) Xarel-lo
d) Sauvignon Blanc
e) Chardonnay
f) Muscat d'Alsace
g) Gewürztraminer
h) all of the above

20. Match the following words, found on Spanish wine labels, with their correct definitions:

1. año	a) rosé
2. blanco	b) sweet
3. cepa	c) made and aged by
4. cosecha	d) bottled by
5. dulce	e) estate-bottled
6. elaborado y envejecido por	f) wine from the owner's own harvest (estate-bottled)
7. embotellado en la bodega	g) dry
8. embotellado en la propiedad	h) harvest
9. embotellado por	i) grape variety
10. producido por	j) bottled at the winery
11. rosado	k) produced by
12. seco	l) year
13. vendimia	m) vintage
14. vino de cosecha propia	n) white

ANSWERS

1. *False. Red, white, and rosé wines are all produced in Rioja.*

2. *c. Sherry is only produced in a delimited district in southern Spain around the city of Jerez de la Frontera.*

3. *True. Each bodega (winemaking concern) blends its wines according to its own "house style." This involves blending various grape varieties from different vineyards or locations within the Rioja region, and it may also involve blending wines from several vintages. Since the art of Rioja winemaking depends on this blending, rather than on the cultivation of any one particular grape variety, the bodega's name on the label is very important.*

4. *b. Cabernet Sauvignon is practically nonexistent in Rioja. Marques de Riscal has about fifty acres of this noble variety, but is one of the few bodegas in Rioja, if not the only one, to use it.*

5. *a. Tempranillo is the major grape variety used in the red wines of Rioja. It often constitutes 50 to 75 percent of the blends.*

6. *a) Rioja Alavesa is the smallest zone.*
b) Rioja Baja is the largest zone.
c) Rioja Alavesa is located on the northeastern bank of the Rio Ebro.

Wines produced in the Rioja Alta and the Rioja Alavesa zones are considered to be the finest; either of these designations may occasionally appear on the labels of wines produced from grapes grown in the specified zone. Wines produced from grapes grown in the Rioja Baja, where the climate is hotter and drier, tend to be rather coarse and higher in alcohol. It is not unusual for bodegas to blend together wines from all three subdistricts, utilizing the individual characteristics of each zone to end up with a better-balanced product.

7. *c. Alavesa is located in the province of Alava, hence its name.*

8. *b. The Rio Oja, a small tributary of the Rio Ebro, joins the main river at Haro and gives the region its name.*

9. *c. Some of the brand names used by bodegas originated from the names of certain Rioja vineyards—Tondonia, Zaco, Paceta, and Pomal, for example—but these wines are also blended from other vineyards, none of which may be the famous vineyard named on the label. As such, they are simply brand names.*

10. *b. When the phylloxera epidemic began devastating the Bordeaux vineyards in the late 1860s, many of the growers moved across the Pyrenees to nearby Rioja, where they were able to continue working. These families returned to Bordeaux as vineyards were replanted, but many of the French winemaking techniques that they introduced during this period are still used in Rioja today.*

11. *d. Oddly enough, eighty-four-gallon barrels made of American oak are called bordelesas. Marimar Torres, a member of the innovative Torres wine family of Penedès, has an interesting theory concerning the traditional use of American oak barrels in Spain, rather than those of French oak. According to Marimar, "Our family has been making wine since the seventeenth century; and if you think about history for a minute, in those days Spain was not exactly a close friend of France. . . . Rather, we were fighting all the time. On the other hand, America had already been discovered by Spain, and the trade between the two countries was flourishing. So, does it not make a lot of sense that we should be aging our wines in casks made of wood from our friend America, rather than from a neighbor with whom we were constantly involved in wars?"*

12. *c. Valdepeñas is produced on the plains of La Mancha around the town of Valdepeñas in central Spain. Red, white, and rosé wines are all produced in this area.*

13. *Extrísimo is a sweet white wine produced as a specialty by the firm of Masia Bach, which is located in the Penedès region of Catalonia. An Extrísimo Seco is also produced, and both are blends of Parallada, Macabeo, and Xarel-lo grapes. Masia Bach, bought by the House of Codorniu in 1975, was founded at the beginning of the century by the Bach brothers, Peter and Raymond. They had made a lot of money in the cotton business, and in that trade the word* extrísimo *was applied to the finest grade of cotton. They borrowed the word for their white wines, which they also considered to be very fine.*

14. *1–b, 2–a, 3–b, 4–a, 5–c.*

15. *c. Bodeguero is the Spanish term for winemaker.*

16. *Clarete is generally a light red wine; tinto is a fuller-bodied, deep ruby-colored wine.*

17. *a. Baix Penedès (Low Penedès) is the area nearest the Mediterranean where the climate is warm and better suited to growing red grapes.*

b. Alt Penedès (High Penedès) is the mountainous area farthest from the sea; elevations here fluctuate from one thousand feet to over twenty-five hundred feet, creating a cool climate that is especially favorable for growing white grapes with high acid levels, an unusual feat in the Mediterranean area.

18. *b. I have never looked into the eyes of a Catalan hare, but I can only suppose that they must be red, a similar color to the Ull de Llebra grape.*

19. *h. They are all used to make white wines in Penedès. Although most Spanish wines are made from traditional Spanish grape varieties, a few progressive wineries, like Torres and Jean Leon in the Penedès region, have succeeded in introducing several "noble" French grape varieties to select vineyard sites. Cabernet Sauvignon, Cabernet Franc, and Pinot Noir are among the red varieties that have proven to grow well. Their aristocratic presence has consequently raised certain Penedès wines to a superior level. Masia Bach is another Penedès firm with experimental plots of some of these finer grape varieties.*

Of course, the desire to improve upon tradition is not restricted to the region of Penedès. Growers in other areas are also laying out experimental plots, primarily for blending purposes. The quintessential Vega Sicilia—made by a formula of secret proportions of Cabernet Sauvignon, Malbec, Merlot, Tinto Fino, and the Albillo-Blanco, perhaps sets the greatest example of what can be achieved when both Spanish and French varieties are skillfully combined.

20. *1–1, 2–n, 3–i, 4–h, 5–b, 6–c, 7–j, 8–e, 9–d, 10–k, 11–a, 12–g, 13–m, 14–f.*

Hungary

The Doctor he gave me some Spanish quinine:
All his powders were wasted, my body was lean,
The Hungarian cure made me feel hale and fine,
I was cured by my cellar's fifteen-year-old wine!
Jozsef Gvadanyi (1725–1801)

1. What is the most famous Hungarian wine?

2. If you found a bottle of Badacsonyi Szurkebarat, you would know that it was produced from:
a) the white Badacsonyi grape grown in Szurkebarat
b) the red Badacsonyi grape grown in Szurkebarat
c) the white Szurkebarat grape grown in Badacsony
d) the red Szurkebarat grape grown in Badacsony

3. Indicate which of the following wines are white (W) and which are red (R):
1. Nemes Kadarka
2. Leanyka
3. Somloi Furmint
4. Debroi Harslevelu
5. Szekszardi Voros
6. Badacsonyi Keknyelu
7. Villanyi Burgundi
8. Magyar Voros

4. The word Voros on a Hungarian wine means that it is:
a) red
b) white
c) rosé

5. Of Hungary's four major wine regions, The Great Plain (Alfold), Northern Transdanubia, Southern Transdanubia, and Northern Hungary,

a) which produces the bulk of Hungary's commercial wine?

b) where is the famous red wine Egri Bikaver, Bull's Blood of Eger, produced?

c) where is Tokay (Tokaj) produced?

6. If you should find a bottle of Hungarian wine labeled Hajosi Cabernet, you would immediately know that it's:

a) a fake; all Hungarian wines are made from Hungarian grape varieties that are difficult to pronounce

b) almost exclusively made from Cabernet Franc

c) almost exclusively made from Cabernet Sauvignon

d) almost exclusively made from Médoc Noir (Merlot)

7. Many Hungarian grape varieties have characteristic names; match the following varieties with their meanings:

1. Keknyelu	a) lime leaf
2. Szurkebarat	b) young maiden
3. Harsleveu	c) lamb's tail
4. Ezerjo	d) blue stalk
5. Mezesfeher	e) a thousand boons
6. Leanyka	f) Gray Friar
7. Juhfark	g) honey white

8. What is the name of the only agency entitled to export wines from Hungary?

ANSWERS

1. *Tokay (Tokaj), made primarily from the Furmint grape, is known and appreciated the world over.*

2. c. *Hungarian wines are usually labeled with the place-name (the possessive -i added at the end), followed by the grape variety. Szurkebarat (Gray Friar) is the Hungarian name for the French Pinot Gris.*

3. *1–R, 2–W, 3–W, 4–W, 5–R, 6–W, 7–R, 8–R.*

4. *a. red.*

5. *a. The Great Plain (Alfold).*
b. Northern Hungary, where Eger is located.
c. *Northern Hungary, in the specific area of Tokaj-Hegyalja.*

6. *b. Most Hungarian wines labeled Cabernet are made almost entirely from Cabernet Franc.*

7. *1–d, 2–f, 3–a, 4–e, 5–g, 6–b, 7–c.*

8. *Monimpex, the Hungarian Foreign Trading Company, is the only agency that exports Hungarian wines.*

FLIGHT V

South America
Australia
New Zealand
South Africa

South America

Wine Flash . . . A prominent American wine writer highly recommends that white wines from South America be served chilly!

1. Which country is the largest producer of wine in South America?
2. In which province are most of Argentina's vineyards located?
3. What is the significance of a vintage year when it appears on the label of an Argentine wine?
4. What is the dominant grape variety used for production of fine red wines in Argentina?
5. How is the vineyard irrigation system in Argentina used to combat *phylloxera*?
6. What is the principal winegrowing region in Brazil?
7. What is the leading grape variety planted in Brazil?
8. Conde de Foucauld, Granja União, Marjolet, and Acquasantiera are all:
   a) domestic Brazilian grape varieties
   b) wine-producing areas in Brazil
   c) brand names of Brazilian wines
   d) tropical insects that thrive on *vinifera* grapes
   e) none of the above
9. What is the name of Brazil's first and only public college specializing in wine production?

10. What company is the biggest single producer of wines in Brazil?

11. Who is cited as the father of Chilean viticulture?

12. Chilean vines are practically disease-free and have never been ravaged by a phylloxera infestation. True or false?

13. Chile is divided into three viticultural zones. What are they called, and what kind of wine is produced in each?

14. What are the two leading French red-grape varieties planted in Chile?

15. What are the two leading French white-grape varieties planted in Chile?

16. What is another name used for the Malbeck (spelled with a "k" in South America) grape in Chile?

17. What grape of Spanish origin has been grown in Chile for so long that it is accepted as a domestic variety?

18. Which progressive Spanish wine firm has acquired a winery and vineyards in the Curicó Valley (central region) of Chile?

19. Concha y Toro, one of Chile's leading wine firms, is located in one of the best sections of the central region; which?
a) Aconcagua Valley
b) Maipo Valley
c) Curicó Valley

20. There are four categories of export wines in Chile, which are determined by the wine's age. Match the ages below to their corresponding classifications.

1. one year old	a) Reserve
2. two years old	b) Courant
3. four years old	c) Gran Vino
4. six years old or more	d) Special

ANSWERS

1. *Argentina, with an annual production of about 650 million gallons, is the largest producer of wine in South America. In addition, it is the world's fifth largest producer behind the Soviet Union, Spain, France and Italy.*

2. *Over 70 percent of the Argentine vineyards are planted in the Mendoza Province, about seven hundred miles west of Buenos Aires.*

3. *When a vintage year is indicated on the label of an Argentine wine, the year is determined by the average vintage of its contents. A vintage date does not necessarily mean that the wine came from the harvest year indicated, but that it may be a blend of several vintages with an averaged date.*

4. *The Malbeck, a variety that originated in the Bordeaux area of France, dominates production of the best red wines Argentina has to offer.*

5. *Argentine winegrowers use irrigation to rid their vineyards of* phylloxera *by flooding the infected areas for a brief period of time, thereby drowning the pest. Due to a lack of rainfall, most vineyards must be irrigated with water that melts from the snow-capped peaks of the Andes. The water is distributed by means of an extremely complex irrigation network, considered to be one of the best in the world. Oddly enough, some people claim that this network is also responsible for the spread of* phylloxera, *flushing the parasites in its ducts from one region to another.*

6. *Nearly 65 percent of Brazil's wine output comes from the southern state of Rio Grande do Sul. Although Brazil is the largest South American country, most of it is too tropical for growing grapes.*

7. *The Isabella, a native American grape, along with other* Vitis labrusca *hybrids, has dominated the vineyards of Brazil since 1860. American varieties constituted 84 percent of Brazilian production in 1980. During the mid-1970s, however, a trend toward increasing the acreage of the noble European varieties,* Vitis vinifera, *took hold. Although the cultivation of* vinifera *remains limited, these finer grape varieties have generated a renewed interest in the Brazilian wine industry.*

8. *c. brand names of Brazilian wines.*

9. *Colegio de Viticultura e Enologia (CVE) began classes in grape growing and winemaking in 1960 in the city of Bento Gonçalves and now matriculates about two hundred students a year.*

10. *Dreher-Heublein (Heublein do Brazil Comércio e Industria, Ltd.) of São Paulo, which in 1981 crushed 24 million liters of wine through Dreher S.A. Vinhos e Champanhas of Bento Gonçalves, is the largest producer in Brazil. Dreher is one of the oldest wine companies in the country, and Heublein bought the family-owned business in 1973.*

11. *Silvestre Ochagavia is referred to as the father of Chilean viticulture. In 1851 he contracted the services of a French viticulturist who brought the first French vine cuttings into Chile, thus launching a vast improvement and expansion of the Chilean wine industry.*

12. *True. Although* phylloxera *has taken its toll of vineyards in other South American countries, it has never spread to Chile. The massive Andean mountains bordering Chile on the east and the Atacama desert in the north have obstructed the parasite's entry into the country. In addition, strict agricultural border inspections have thus far been successful in blocking its entry by that route. The result is that even the most susceptible vines in Chile may be grown on their own tender rootstocks.*

13. *Chile's winegrowing regions include the northern region, producing mostly sweet, fortified wine types; the central region, producing the best table wines in South America; and the southern region, producing ordinary bulk wine.*

14. *Cabernet Sauvignon and Cabernet Franc are the leading French red-grape varieties, producing Chilean wines similar in style to good regional Bordeaux.*

15. *Sémillon and Sauvignon Blanc are neck and neck for the leading white French varieties in Chile.*

16. *Cot is another name used for the Malbeck grape in Chile.*

17. *The Pais, a red grape of lesser quality, is not only accepted as a domestic variety, but also accounts for over 50 percent of the vines grown in Chile, producing large quantities of bulk wine in the southern region.*

18. *In 1979 the firm of Torres, based in the Penedés region of Spain, purchased the Chilean vineyards and winery of the Ahrex family, established in 1904. The land is planted with about 150 acres of Sauvignon Blanc and 100 acres of Cabernet Franc, all grown on their own rootstocks. Two varietal wines are produced and are sold under the brand name Miguel Torres Chile.*

19. *b. Concha y Toro's vineyards are planted in the Maipo Valley.*

20. *1–b, 2–d, 3–a, 4–c.*

Australia

1. Which months mark the beginning and end of harvest time in Australia?

2. What is the most widely planted red-wine grape in Australia?

3. How are white Australian wines labeled when they are made from the "true" Johannisberg Riesling grape variety?

4. Many vines in Australia are still grown on their original rootstocks. True or false?

5. Which is the largest wine-producing state in Australia?

6. Match each wine region listed below with the state in which it's located:

1. Barossa Valley
2. Clare
3. Coonawarra
4. Hunter River Valley
5. Milawa
6. Mt. Barker
7. Margaret River
8. Swan Valley
9. Yarra Valley

a) New South Wales
b) South Australia
c) Victoria
d) Western Australia

7. What Australian winery is associated with the Robert Mondavi Winery in California?

8. Dominique Portet—brother of Bernard Portet, who is the winemaker at Clos Du Val in the Napa Valley—is the winemaker for what Australian winery?

9. One of Australia's greatest red wines is Grange Hermitage, produced by Penfolds; how did this wine come by its name?

10. Who is acknowledged as the father of Australian viticulture?

11. What was the name of the vineyard developed by James Busby from a grant of two thousand acres in the Hunter Valley?

12. If you should notice the phrase "anaerobic fermented" on a bottle of Australian wine, you would know that it was:
    a) barrel fermented
    b) sparkling
    c) made by carbonic maceration
    d) a late-harvest wine

ANSWERS

1. *Harvest time in the Southern Hemisphere begins in the early part of the year; in Australia it usually begins in January in the hotter regions and finishes in the higher, cooler regions in May.*

2. *The Shiraz, considered to be a strain of the "true" Syrah derived from the Hermitage variety of the Rhône region in France, is the most widely planted red-wine grape.*

3. *Wines made from the "true" Riesling are labeled "Rhine Riesling." Those labeled merely "Riesling" may be made from the Sémillon grape.*

4. *True. In Australia, only the state of Victoria was ravaged by* phylloxera *in the late 1800s. As a result, much of the rest of the country is still able to grow vines on their own rootstocks without fear of infestation.*

5. *South Australia is the premier wine-producing state, providing over 50 percent of the country's production.*

6. *1–b, 2–b, 3–b, 4–a, 5–c, 6–d, 7–d, 8–d, 9–c.*

7. *Robert Mondavi has a financial interest in the Leeuwin Estate Winery at Margaret River in Western Australia. He acts as consultant for the winery, which produces Rhine Riesling, Chardonnay, Cabernet Sauvignon, and Traminer.*

8. *Dominique Portet is the winemaker for Taltarni Vineyards at Moonambe in Victoria.*

9. *The wine is named after "The Grange," the old cottage of the winery's founder, Dr. Penfold, at Magill in South Australia.*

10. *James Busby is often called the father of Australian viticulture. His contributions to the industry include the introduction into Australia of a large vine collection that he obtained in Europe in 1831,* *and the writing of two treatises on cultivating vines and making wine.*

11. *James Busby named his vineyard Kirkton.*

12. *c. Australian wines made by carbonic maceration are sometimes labeled "anaerobic ferемented."*

New Zealand

1. Generally speaking, the climate of New Zealand's wine-growing areas is similar to that of:
   a) Spain
   b) Australia
   c) Italy
   d) Germany

2. The stony alluvial plains of the Marlborough wine region on the South Island are similar to which premium wine area in California?
   a) Napa Valley
   b) Sonoma
   c) Livermore Valley
   d) San Luis Obispo

3. What grape variety is used to make wines labeled as Riesling Sylvaner in New Zealand?
   a) Rhine Riesling
   b) Sylvaner
   c) Müller-Thurgau
   d) all of the above

4. What is the most widely planted wine grape in New Zealand?

5. What is the name of New Zealand's oldest existing winery?

6. Montana, Corbans, McWilliams, Glenvale, Penfolds, and Cooks are the names of:
   a) hybrid grape varieties developed in New Zealand
   b) New Zealand's major wine-producing regions
   c) suburbs in Auckland

d) the six large firms that account for two-thirds of New Zealand's wine output

7. Matawhero, a small premium winery with a particular reputation for Gewürztraminer, is located in which of the following major wine regions of New Zealand?
a) Gisborne (Poverty Bay)
b) Hawke Bay
c) Auckland
d) Marlborough (Blenheim)
e) South Auckland (Te Kauwhata)

8. What New Zealand winery is so modern that is has been dubbed the "space age winery" by visitors?

ANSWERS

1. *d. Germany. New Zealand is basically a cool-climate wine-growing area.*

2. *c. Livermore Valley.*

3. *c. Müller-Thurgau is the correct name for the grape varietal known as Riesling Sylvaner in New Zealand.*

4. *The Riesling Sylvaner (Müller-Thurgau) is the most widely grown wine grape in New Zealand.*

5. *The Mission at Greenmeadows, Hawke Bay, was established in 1865 by Catholic priests of the Marist Order and still operates today as New Zealand's oldest winery.*

6. *d. the six large firms that account for two-thirds of New Zealand's wine output.*

7. *a. Gisborne.*

8. *Cook's Te Kauwhata Winery, owned by Cook's New Zealand Wines, Ltd., is called the "space age winery."*

South Africa

1. Who is responsible for bringing the first vines to South Africa on a ship from the Dutch East India Company in 1655?

2. What is the most widely planted Cape wine grape variety?

3. What important red-grape variety is indigenous to South Africa?

4. South Africans have adopted traditional local names for certain European grape varieties. Match each of the following local names with its correct European counterpart.

1. Steen	a) Cinsaut
2. White French	b) Chenin Blanc
3. Green grape	c) Palomino Fino
4. Hermitage	d) Muscat of Alexandria
5. Hanepoot	e) Sémillon

5. In what year did South Africa adopt an appellation system by introducing the W.O. (Wines of Origin) seal?
   a) 1910
   b) 1964
   c) 1973
   d) 1980

6. What is the significance of the W.O.S. (Wines of Origin Superior) seal on a bottle of Cape wine?

7. Of the two main wine regions in South Africa, the Coastal Belt in the southwest and Little Karoo in the east, which produces the finer table wines?

ANSWERS

1. *The first governor and founder of the Cape settlement, Johan van Riebeeck, brought the first vines into South Africa.*

2. *The Steen (Chenin Blanc) is the most widely planted wine grape variety in South Africa.*

3. *The Pinotage is indigenous to South Africa. It was developed in 1925 by Professor A. I. Perold, who successfully crossed Pinot Noir and Cinsaut (Hermitage). It was Professor C. J. Theron, however, who propagated the new seedlings and put the vine through its paces.*

4. *1–b, 2–c, 3–e, 4–a, 5–d.*

5. *c. 1973.*

6. *The W.O.S. seal is a designation for a superior-quality wine made from a single grape variety, if the variety is stated on the label.*

7. *The best wines come from the Coastal Belt, which has a better climate for grape growing, due to the influence of the Atlantic Ocean. In the warmer Little Karoo, where the vineyards are irrigated, the wines produced are more ordinary.*

FLIGHT VI

Champagne
Other Sparkling Wines
Dessert and Fortified Wines

Champagne

I drink it when I'm happy and when I'm sad. Sometimes I drink it when I'm alone. When I have company, I consider it obligatory. I trifle with it if I'm not hungry and drink it when I am. Otherwise, I never touch it—unless I'm thirsty.

Madame Bollinger (1899–1977)
"La Grande Dame du Champagne"

I like Champagne, because it always tastes as though my foot's asleep.

Art Buchwald

1. Champagne is a blended wine. True or false?
2. What are the only three grape varieties permitted in Champagne?
3. In a classic Champagne blend, the wine will be pressed from:
   a) 70 percent red grapes and 30 percent white grapes
   b) 50 percent red grapes and 50 percent white grapes
   c) 10 percent red grapes and 90 percent white grapes
4. What is "Blanc de Blancs" Champagne?
5. In which specific area are Chardonnay grapes grown for Champagne?
   a) the Mountain of Reims
   b) the Valley of the Marne
   c) the Côte des Blancs
6. Champagne sparkles because:

a) it is made in the spring
b) carbon dioxide is trapped when the wines are blended
c) it is shaken vigorously before being corked
d) a second fermentation takes place in the bottle

7. What famous monk is acclaimed for harnessing the sparkle in Champagne?

8. Who invented the system of *remuage* (riddling), turning bottles of sparkling wine by hand to position the sediment for removal?

9. What is the name for the A-frame riddling rack used in the *méthode champenoise?*

10. Approximately how many pounds of grapes does it take to produce one bottle of Champagne?

11. What specific type of soil contributes to the unique character and flavor of grapes grown in Champagne?

12. The term "Champagne" describes:
a) a wine
b) a region of France
c) a method of producing sparkling wine
d) all of the above

13. A vintage Champagne must be made from:
a) at least 51 percent of the wine from the designated vintage
b) at least 80 percent of the wine from the designated vintage
c) 100 percent of the wine from the designated vintage
d) no fixed percentage, since it depends on the producer's blend

14. Vintage Champagnes are only produced in odd-numbered years. True or false?

15. Number the following designations found on Champagne labels from the driest #1 to the sweetest #5:

Extra Dry
Brut
Doux
Demi-Sec
Sec

16. What do the terms *Brut Sauvage, Ultra Brut, Zéro Brut, Brut Integral,* and *English Cuvée* indicate on a label of Champagne?

17. Why the punt (bottom indentation) in Champagne bottles?
    a) to concentrate the sediment before disgorging
    b) to reduce internal pressure
    c) to aid in stacking bottles
    d) to provide a thumb-grip when pouring Champagne

18. How much wine does a Jeroboam hold?

19. Because of their large size, bottles larger than Jeroboams are not used for fermenting Champagne. The larger bottles are filled from a number of standard ones in which the wine is fermented. A standard bottle holds 750 ml. Match the following bottles with the quantity they hold:

1) Balthazar	a) 6 bottles
2) Methuselah	b) 8 bottles
3) Nebuchadnezzar	c) 12 bottles
4) Rehoboam	d) 16 bottles
5) Salmanazar	e) 20 bottles

20. Number the following twelve steps for making Champagne in their correct order.

pressing grapes
dégorgement
blending the cuvée
harvesting
labeling
dosage de tirage
dosage or liqueur d'expédition
first fermentation
remuage (riddling)
recorking
épluchage
second fermentation

21. Several major Champagne houses bottle a "tête de cuvée" which represents their very best wine. Match the following Champagne firms with their best Champagnes:

1. Laurent Perrier	a) Cristal
2. Louis Roederer	b) Dom Pérignon
3. Moët & Chandon	c) Comtes de Champagne
4. Taittinger	d) Grand Siècle

22. What was the first commercial vintage of Dom Pérignon, and where did it make its debut?

23. Which Champagne house is the official Champagne sponsor for all Grand Prix races throughout the world?

24. What was Sir Winston Churchill's favorite Champagne?

25. What is the significance of the initials "r.m." on a Champagne label?

26. In Ian Fleming's novel *Casino Royale,* which Champagne did the hero James Bond consider to be the finest in the world?

27. What is Côteaux Champenois?

28. What were the still wines produced in Champagne called, prior to the creation of the Côteaux Champenois appellation?

29. What is Crémant?

ANSWERS

1. *True. Non-vintage Champagne is a blend of wines from several years; vintage Champagne is a blend of wines from one superior year.*

2. *Pinot Noir (red), Pinot Meunier (red), and Chardonnay (white) are the only three grape varieties permitted in Champagne.*

3. *a. 70 percent red grapes and 30 percent white grapes.*

4. *Blanc de Blancs is a light, elegant Champagne produced exclusively from Chardonnay grapes.*

5. *c. the Côte des Blancs.*

6. *d. a second fermentation takes place in the bottle.*

7. *Dom Pérignon (1638–1715), a blind Benedictine monk who was the cellarmaster at the Abbey of Hautvillers in the diocese of Reims, is the man who captured the bubbles in Champagne. According to legend, he noticed that the white wines of Champagne refermented in the spring and developed a natural sparkle. Until this time, ineffective bottle stoppers were made of wooden pegs and oil-soaked cotton wadding. Dom Pérignon developed the use of stronger bottles and airtight cork closures tied down with string to capture the bubbles in the wine.*

8. Remuage *was first devised in the nineteenth century by Madame Veuve Clicquot,* née *Ponsardin (1777–1866). After pondering the problem of sediment removal, she had several holes cut into a large table and placed the bottles in the holes upside-down. Although much of the sediment dropped in this position, in some cases it was stubborn and wouldn't budge until the bottles were given a gentle turning shake. This method was named* remuage *(moving around) and was later refined.*

9. *A-frame riddling racks are called pupitres.*

10. *It takes approximately 3.5 pounds of grapes to produce a bottle of Champagne.*

11. *Chalk (Kimmeridge clay) is the major soil element contributing to the uniqueness of Champagne grapes and the flavor they impart to the wine.*

12. *d. all of the above.*

13. *b. at least 80 percent of the wine from the designated vintage.*

14. *False. 1928, 1934, 1952, 1962, 1964, 1966, 1970, and 1976 are examples of even-numbered vintage years in Champagne. One should also remember that there is no such thing as a vintage year for the entire Champagne region. The individual Champagne houses determine whether or not they will bottle a vintage Champagne in any given year, the decision being made not at the time of harvest, but after the wines have aged sufficiently to display their ultimate qualities. In some cases it may take seven years before a house is ready to declare a vintage Champagne.*

15. *1–Brut, 2–Extra Dry, 3–Sec, 4–Demi-Sec, 5–Doux.*

16. *A Champagne labeled with one of these terms will have little or no dosage (sweetening liqueur) added, indicating extreme dryness.*

17. *b. to reduce internal pressure.*

To console those romantics who selected d. for their answer, the Champagne News and Information Bureau has provided a charming story. In restaurants of the Champagne region, and in the dining rooms of the great Champagne firms, wine stewards customarily pour Champagne with the thumb in the punt of the bottle, and fingers supporting it along its length. As one of them explains, "one holds a bottle of red wine by the neck, a woman by the waist, and a bottle of Champagne by the derrière.*"*

18. *A Jeroboam holds 104 ounces, or 3 liters, equal to four standard bottles of Champagne.*

19. *1–d, 2–b, 3–e, 4–a, 5–c.*

20. *1–harvesting; 2–épluchage; 3–pressing grapes; 4–first fermen-*

tation; 5-blending the cuvée; 6-dosage de tirage; 7-second fermentation; 8-remuage; 9-dégorgement; 10-dosage d'expédition; 11-recorking; 12-labeling.

21. *1-d, 2-a, 3-b, 4-c.*

22. *Dom Pérignon was first launched commercially with a 1921 vintage, making its debut, oddly enough, on the American market, and not in France, in the mid-1930s. It was not until 1949 that Dom Pérignon was introduced into the French market; and then with the 1943 vintage commemorating the bicentenary of Maison Moët & Chandon.*

As a result, the French missed out on the vintages of 1921, 1928, 1929, 1934, and 1937.

23. *Moët & Chandon is the official Champagne sponsor for all Grand Prix races.*

24. *Pol Roger was Sir Winston Churchill's favorite Champagne. He liked it so much that he named one of his race horses Pol Roger.*

25. *"r.m."* (récoltants-manipulants) *on a Champagne label indicates that the wine was produced by a grower who retained some of his grapes to make his own Champagne. Of the sixteen thousand growers in Champagne, about five thousand fall into this group. Although most r.m. Champagne is usually sold only to customers in France and a few neighboring countries, these bottles can occasionally be found in the United States.*

26. *In the book* Casino Royale, *Bond remarks that Taittinger's Brut Blanc de Blancs '43 was "probably the finest Champagne in the world."*

27. *Côteaux Champenois is the appellation created in 1975 for the still (non-sparkling) wines made in the Champagne region of France. Most Côteaux is white, but some still red wine is also produced, the most famous of which comes from the village of Bouzy.*

28. *Until 1975 the still wines of Champagne were labeled Vin Nature de la Champagne.*

29. *Crémant (French for "creaming") is a lightly sparkling white or rosé wine with about half as much fizz as Champagne. It is made by the méthode champenoise, but the amount of sugar added in the* *dosage de tirage prior to the second fermentation is reduced, resulting in a sparkling wine that contains from three to six atmospheres of pressure; Champagne contains six or more atmospheres.*

In addition to the crémants of Champagne—the best known of which is Crémant de Cramant made by Mumm, a new Crémant appellation was created in 1975 for certain bottle-fermented lightly sparkling wines (white and rosé only) produced outside the Champagne region. There are at present three crémants entitled to the new appellation: Crémant d'Alsace, Crémant de Bourgogne, and Crémant de Loire.

Sparkling Wines of the World

The saucer-shaped "coupe" glass, considered by many to be a poor vessel, badly suited to serving or drinking Champagne, originated as a porcelain mold of Marie Antoinette's breast. The Queen adored Champagne and the glass was a gallant salute to her good taste. In favoring the tulip or flute shaped glass because it better retains the sparkle and aroma of the wine, connoisseurs suggest the saucer-shaped glass be used either for sherbert or by "those who like their Champagne and their women flat."

Champagne News and Information Bureau

1. What is France's second largest sparkling-wine region after Champagne?

2. Who produced:
a) America's first sparkling wine, and what was it called?
b) California's first sparkling wine, and what was it called?
c) New York's first sparkling wine, and what was it called?

3. In 1950, when the wine competition at the California State Fair in Sacramento was opened to entries from the United States and abroad, what Champagne or sparkling wine won the gold medal?

4. What sparkling wine did Richard Nixon take along on his trip to China in 1972?

5. Which Schramsberg bubbly is closest in style to the traditional French Champagne blend of two-thirds red grapes and one-third white?
   a) Blanc de Blancs
   b) Blanc de Noirs
   c) Crémant
   d) Cuvée de Pinot
   e) Reserve Champagne

6. Sparkling wines made by the traditional méthode champenoise, or Champagne method, are produced in many countries, including Italy, Germany, Spain, and the United States, as well as France. Who is the world's largest single producer of sparkling wines made by the Champagne method?
   a) Korbel (Sonoma, California)
   b) Domaine Chandon (Napa Valley, California)
   c) Great Western (Hammondsport, New York)
   d) Martini & Rossi (Piedmont, Italy)
   e) Fürst von Metternich (Germany)
   f) Codorniu (San Sadurní de Noya, Spain)
   g) Moët & Chandon (Épernay, France)

ANSWERS

1. *Saumur, in the Loire Valley, is the second largest sparkling-wine region in France. Saumur's output, all méthode champenoise, is approximately 12.5 million bottles per year. The Champagne region, with a capacity of 250 million bottles, is the largest.*

2. *a) In 1842, Nicholas Longworth produced America's first sparkling wine at Cincinnati, Ohio; it was called Sparkling Catawba.*

b) California's first sparkler was produced at Los Angeles by the Sainsevain brothers, Jean Louis and Pierre; it was called Sparkling California and was made from Mission grapes. In 1856 they sent a case of this wine to President James Buchanan, who claimed in his thank-you letter that it was "the most agreeable American wine I have yet drunk and gives promise that California is destined ere long to become a great wine producing country."

c) In 1865 the Pleasant Valley Wine Company, known today as Great Western, produced New York's first sparkling wine at Hammondsport; it, too, was orginally called Sparkling Catawba. In 1870, after tasting this wine, horticulturist Marshall P. Wilder declared it to be "the great champagne of the Western world." His remark gave Great Western its name.

3. *Gold Seal's Charles Fournier Brut Champagne from New York State struck gold at the California State Fair in 1950. This fair has since been closed to entries outside California.*

4. *Nixon took twenty-eight cases of California's famed Schramsberg Champagne to China in 1972.*

5. *b. Schramsberg Cellars' Blanc de Noirs is the closest in style to the traditional French blend. Schramsberg was the first in California, in the early 1960s, to use Pinot Noir for sparkling wines.*

6. *f. Maison Moët & Chandon is the largest producer of true Champagne, but it may come as a considerable surprise to learn* *that the world's largest producer of sparkling wines made by the méthode champenoise is an old established Spanish firm called Codorniu. Their estate, in the provinces of Barcelona and Lerida, is twenty thousand acres in area, or about one-third the size of the entire Champagne district in France. They sell about three million cases of cava (the Spanish term for méthode champenoise wines) per year and have sixteen miles of man-made caves, built on five underground levels, which contain about 100 million bottles of sparkling wine at any given time. Interestingly, Moët & Chandon's underground cellars are even larger than Codorniu's, measuring eighteen miles in length.*

Dessert and Fortified Wines

To taste a fine old Layon is a memorable experience. Its rich bouquet suggests fruit, hazelnuts and peaches with a delicate hint of flowers, matching its concentration of flavor with elegance. An underlying flintiness prevents cloying.

Peter F. Wilkins

1. Wines such as Sherry and Port are usually fortified by adding:
   a) a mixture of alcohol and unfermented grape must
   b) brandy, which increases their alcoholic content up to 17 to 21 percent
   c) a syrup of brandy and sugar, which raises their alcoholic content and degree of sweetness
   d) a mixture of alcohol and water
2. Can you name three vintage years for Sherry?
3. The natural yeast that mysteriously develops on the surface of certain Sherries and makes Fino different from Oloroso is called:
   a) venencia
   b) Amontillado
   c) flor
4. Cream Sherry results when sweet wine made from Pedro Ximenez (PX) grapes is blended with:
   a) Amontillado
   b) Oloroso
   c) Fino

5. The solera system is a means of:
   a) blending old wine with young
   b) blending one style of wine with another
   c) aging wines with solar heating units
   d) baking the wine to achieve a characteristically nutty flavor

6. Rank the following styles of Sherry from driest (#1) to sweetest (#5).
   Amontillado
   Cream
   Fino
   Manzanilla
   Oloroso

7. Which of the Sherries in Question 6 should be served chilled for the fullest enjoyment?

8. In Jerez de la Frontera, who is acknowledged as the greatest Sherry authority of them all and is called by the nickname La Nariz ("the nose")?

9. In Edgar Allan Poe's *The Cask of Amontillado,* the villian, Montresor, entices Fortunato into his wine vaults by inviting him to evaluate a "pipe" of Amontillado. What is the error in Montresor's invitation?

10. Port produced from a single vintage and bottled after four to six years' aging in wood is called:
    a) Vintage Port
    b) Late-bottled Vintage Port
    c) Port of the Vintage

11. How many liters are there in a Douro Port pipe?

12. Occasionally a Vintage Port will be made only from the grapes of a single vineyard. Match the following single-vineyard Ports with their shippers:

1. Qunita do Malvedos	a) Offley
2. Vargellas	b) Warre
3. Roêda	c) Graham

4. Boa Vista
5. Eira Velha
6. Corte
7. Sibio
8. Cavadinha

d) Royal Oporto
e) Delaforce
f) Taylor
g) Croft
h) Cockburn

13. What happens when ripe grapes develop the fungus known as noble rot?
a) Poisonous purple lesions develop on their skins, and they become useless for winemaking.
b) They shrivel, and as a result their sugar levels and flavor elements become extremely concentrated.
c) A royal-blue mold forms on their skins, and the resulting wines have a unique cheesy flavor.
d) They fall off the vine and must be harvested by hand.

14. What is the mycological name for noble rot?
a) *Phylloxera vastatrix*
b) Trockenbeerenauslese
c) *Vitis cinerea*
d) *Botrytis cinerea*

15. Concerning the 1855 Classification of Sauternes and Barsac,
a) What was the only vineyard ranked as a Premier Grand Cru (first great growth)?
b) How many vineyards were rated?
c) What classified property, a second growth, decided to uproot its vines after the 1975 vintage?
d) What was the name of Château Guiraud back in 1855?

16. On which of the following grape varieties is noble rot desirable?
a) Sémillon
b) Sauvignon Blanc
c) Chardonnay
d) Riesling
e) Cabernet Sauvignon
f) Chenin Blanc

17. Match the wine with its place of origin:

1. Picolit
2. Muscat Beaumes de Venice
3. Catawba Ice Wine
4. Banyuls
5. Marsala
6. Moscatel de Setúbal
7. Mavrodaphne
8. Vino Santo
9. Commandaria

a) France
b) Italy
c) Portugal
d) Greece
e) United States
f) Cyprus
g) Sicily

18. Which California winery does not belong in the following list?
a) Ficklin
b) Jordan
c) Quady
d) The Christian Brothers
e) J. W. Morris
f) Woodbury

19. The wines of Madeira, a small Portuguese island off the coast of North Africa, are produced in four basic styles: Verdelho, Malmsey, Sercial, and Bual (Boal).
a) What do the names represent?
b) Which is the driest?
c) Which is the sweetest?

20. What unique process is used in the production of Madeira?

21. In Shakespeare's *King Henry IV,* Falstaff is accused of selling his soul for a cup of:
a) Port
b) Sherry
c) Madeira

22. Tokaji Aszú, a luscious, tangy dessert wine from Hungary, is made in a special way. Fill in the numbered blanks, using the words listed below, or an appropriate number, to complete the story. Some words will be used more than once.
a) aszú
b) gönc

c) puttonyos
d) Furmint
e) Botrytis cinerea
f) select a number

After the normal harvest, (1)______ grapes are left on the vines to develop (2)______. When shriveled with mold, the grapes are called (3)______. They are selectively picked and put into wooden butts, known as (4)______, which hold about (5)______ liters. A certain number of these (6)______ are then added to the must of the grapes from the normal harvest, and the lot is fermented together in a 120–140 liter cask, which is called a (7)______. The more (8)______ added to the (9)______, the sweeter and richer the resulting wine will be. Bottles of Tokaji Aszú are labeled with the number of (10)______ used to enrich the wines. (11)______ (12)______ is the sweetest grade available.

23. What California winery was the first to use the solera system to produce its sherry?

ANSWERS

1. *b. Brandy is added, to arrest the fermentation process in order to retain natural sweetness in the wine, and/or to increase the alcoholic content.*

2. *Sherry is always a blended wine from several vintages; as such, vintage sherries do not exist.*

3. *c. A wine that wants to be a Fino mysteriously develops a thick coating of flor (the Spanish word for flower) on its surface. A wine that wants to be an Amontillado also forms flor, but it is thinner than on the Fino. When no flor develops on the surface of the wine, it becomes an Oloroso. (A venencia is a long tool, somewhat like a dipstick with a cup at the end, used for drawing a sample of Sherry from the barrel.)*

4. *b. Oloroso.*

5. *a. Blending wines of different vintages insures a uniform style of wine year after year. Although it originated in the Sherry district, the solera system is commonly used for blending other wines as well, including Port, Madeira, some Marsala and also brandies.*

6. *1–Manzanilla, 2–Fino, 3–Amontillado, 4–Oloroso, 5–Cream.*

7. *Manzanillas and Finos should be served chilled. This is how the Jerezanos drink them. Amontillado may also be chilled, but this wine, along with Oloroso and Cream, is traditionally enjoyed at room temperature. However, all three of these sweeter styles have enough body to stand up to ice and are very refreshing when served on the rocks.*

8. *Don José Ignacio Domecq, Sr. is known as "La Nariz."*

9. *Amontillado is a style of Sherry, and Sherry comes not in pipes, but in butts. A pipe is a cask of Port.*

10. *b. Late-bottled Vintage Port, or LBV. Vintage Port is also the product of a single year, but it is bottled within two years of the harvest and then matured in bottle. Port of the Vintage refers to an old Tawny from a specific year, often refreshed with younger wines and bottled after many years' aging in wood.*

11. *There are approximately 534 liters in a Douro Port pipe.*

12. *1–c, 2–f, 3–g, 4–a, 5–h, 6–e, 7–d, 8–b.*

13. *b. Wines produced from these grapes are unctuously rich and naturally sweet. Noble rot is essential to the production of the world's greatest sweet white wines, including Sauternes and Barsacs from Bordeaux, Tokaji Aszú from Hungary, and the best Beerenauslesen and Trockenbeerenauslesen from Germany. California and New York State have also produced some fine examples.*

14. *d.* Botrytis cinerea *is the botanical name for noble rot. In France, the fungus is called* pourriture noble, *in Germany* edelfäule, *and in Italy* muffa nobile.
Vitis cinerea, *by the way, is a native American grape species that produces the Ashy-Leaf (Sweet Winter) grape.*

15. *a) Château d'Yquem was the only vineyard rated as a Premier Grand Cru, and today its wines remain unique among the world's greatest.*

b) One first great growth, nine first growths, and eleven second growths were classified in 1855. Because some of these properties were later divided, the list now counts one first great growth, eleven first growths, and fifteen second growths. Divided properties are shown bracketed in the list below, indicating that they were once a single château.

Premier Grand Cru (first great growth)

Ch. d'Yquem (Sauternes)

Premiers Crus (first growths)

Ch. La Tour Blanche (Bommes)
{ *Ch. Lafaurie-Peyraguey (Bommes)*
{ *Clos Haut-Peyraguey (Bommes)*
Ch. Rayne-Vigneau (Bommes)
Ch. Suduiraut (Preignac)
Ch. Coutet (Barsac)
Ch. Climens (Barsac)
Ch. Guiraud (Sauternes)

Ch. Rieussec (Farques)
Ch. Rabaud-Promis (Bommes)
Ch. Sigalas-Rabaud (Bommes)

Deuxiemes Crus (second growths)

**Ch. de Myrat (Barsac)*
Ch. Doisy-Däene (Brasac)
Ch. Doisy-Dubroca (Brasac)
Ch. Doisy-Védrines (Barsac)
Ch. d'Arche (Sauternes)
Ch. Filhot (Sauternes)
Ch. Broustet (Barsac)
Ch. Nairac (Barsac)
Ch. Caillou (Barsac)
Ch. Suau (Barsac)
Ch. de Malle (Preignac)
Ch. Romer-Fargesin (Fargues)
Ch. Romer-Hayot (Fargues)
Ch. Lamothe (Sauternes)
Ch. Lamothe-Bergey (Sauternes)

Note: Château Peixotto, classified as a second growth in 1855, is now incorporated into the vineyard of Rabaud-Promis and, therefore, is excluded from this list.

c) Château de Myrat (Barsac) pulled up its vines and is no longer in production. The steady decline in demand for sweet wines, the high cost and uncertainty of Sauternes' production, and a series of poor vintages over nearly two decades had a great deal to do with their decision. It's a pity that such valuable land now lies barren within the heart of this great wine-producing region.

d) At the time of the 1855 Classification, Château Guiraud was known as Château Bayle.

16. *a,b,d,f. Noble rot is beneficial only to certain white grapes. The few wines occasionally made with botrytis-infected Chardonnay grapes have proven only to be oddities, never fine.*

17. *1–b, 2–a, 3–e, 4–a, 5–g, 6–c, 7–d, 8–b, 9–f.*

18. *b. Jordan Vineyard and Winery, located in Alexander Valley, produces only table wines of exceptionally high quality and breed. The others are all noted for their outstanding ports.*

*No longer in production.

19. *a) Verdelho, Malmsey, Sercial, and Bual (Boal) are the names for the grape varieties used in these wines.*

b) Sercial is the driest.

c) Malmsey is the sweetest.

20. *The wines are baked in large, heated vats for a minimum of three months at a temperature no higher than 122°F. This unique "heat treatment," which contributes to Madeira's distinctive flavor, was orginally discovered when the wine was first shipped to other countries. The long sea voyages, often through tropical climates, seemed to improve the wines by the very fact that they were stored in the hot, humid holds of the ships. The baking process is meant to simulate the beneficial effects of the old sea voyages.*

21. *c. From Act I, Scene II: "Jack, how agrees the devil and thee about thy soul, that thou soldest him on Good Friday last for a cup of Madeira and a cold capon's leg?"*

22. *1–Furmint, 2–Botrytis cinerea, 3–aszú, 4–puttonyos, 5–thirty, 6–puttonyos, 7–gönc, 8–puttonyos, 9–gönc, 10–puttonyos, 11–five, 12–puttonyos.*

23. *The Louis M. Martini Winery is believed to be the first in California to use the solera system. The Martini solera was built in 1936, but some of their blends date back to 1922.*

FLIGHT VII

Odd Bin Lots

Hollywood and the Vine

I Am A Vineyard

Odd Bin Lots

After a fine meal, a wine connoisseur was offered some grapes for dessert.

"Thank you," said he, pushing the dish away from him, "But I am not in the habit of taking my wine in pills."

A. Brillat-Savarin
The Physiology of Taste

1. What is the difference between a wine labeled "English wine" and one labeled "British wine"?
2. If you wanted to buy a Swiss wine made from the "true" Riesling grape, would you select a bottle labeled "Johannisberg" or one labeled "Riesling"?
3. In cooking, the alcohol content of wine evaporates, and only the aroma and flavor of the wine is imparted to the food. True or false?
4. It is advisable to use the same style and color of wine for cooking as for drinking with the meal, so that there won't be a flavor clash. True or false?
5. With two exceptions, all wines should be stored horizontally so that the cork is kept in contact with the wine and therefore does not dry out; what are the two exceptions?
6. Wine "breathes" through its cork and has a tendency to absorb odors from the air. True or false?
7. Why do some table wine bottles have a punt (an indentation underneath)?
8. What is the difference between a vertical tasting and a

horizontal tasting? Match the terms with their correct definitions.

a) comparing several wines from one particular vintage and produced from the same grape variety; for example, Chalone Chardonnay '81, Matanzas Creek Chardonnay '81, and Grgich Chardonnay '81

b) comparing several vintages of a particular wine; for example, Wagner Chardonnay '80, '81, and '82

9. What are the two main reasons for decanting a wine?

10. Wines stored in a humid cellar may grow a fungus on the outside of the cork which will indicate that the wine is spoiled. True or false?

11. A wine glass should have a stem in order to keep the heat of your hand from interfering with the temperature of the wine. True or false?

ANSWERS

1. *"English wine" is made from fresh grapes grown in English vineyards. "British wine" is made from grape juice that is imported into Britain from other wine-producing countries.*

2. *Swiss wines labeled "Riesling" may be made only from the "true" Riesling grape. Those labeled "Johannisberg" may be made either from Sylvaner, a lesser variety, or from Riesling. Interestingly, just the opposite is true in California.*

3. *True.*

4. *True.*

5. *Sherry and Madeira are the two exceptions to the rule of horizontal storage. Over a long period of time, the high alcohol content of these wines can eat into the cork and cause some deterioration of the wine. Although Port also has a high alcohol level, those meant for storing should be laid away horizontally and not disturbed, because the sediment crust that forms on the sides of the bottle can be considerable.*

6. *True. For this reason wines should not be stored near goods that emit strong odors. Keep them away from fuels and painting supplies, for example, and avoid lengthy chilling in a refrigerator that smells of onions, garlic, or strong cheese.*

7. *A punt allows the sediment in a wine to concentrate better for decanting.*

8. *Vertical–b, Horizontal–a.*

9. *The two main reasons for decanting a wine are to remove it from its sediment and to allow it to "breathe" (to come into contact with the air).*

10. *False.*

11. *True.*

Hollywood and the Vine

Wine, it's in my veins and I can't get it out.
Burgess Meredith

1. A stately Victorian château bedecked with gables and a veranda that overlooks neatly manicured vineyards provides the exterior setting for the popular television series *Falcon Crest,* produced by Lorimar Productions. This is not an improvised movie set, but a real, honest-to-goodness Napa winery noted for its magnificent Chardonnays. By what name is it known to the wine-wise?
2. "The Vintage Years," the pilot responsible for launching the Falcon Crest series, never aired on television because of a lawsuit. From publicity, however, we know that it was filmed at a prestigious wine château in the Mayacamas Mountains. What winery provided the unique setting?
3. What wine co-starred with Claude Rains, Cary Grant and Ingrid Bergman in Alfred Hitchcock's film *Notorious*?
4. In the television movie *Killer Bees*, starring Gloria Swanson,
   a) what historical wine estate was used for the setting?
   b) who played the role of the Episcopal priest summoned for the heroine's last rites?
   c) what famous movie director has since purchased this fabulous estate and is now marketing wine under its name, coupled with his own?

5. Match the following celebrity wineries and vineyards with their correct locations.
   1. Silverado Vineyards (Lillian Disney)
   2. Pat Paulsen Vineyards (Pat Paulsen)
   3. Niebaum-Copolla Estate (Francis Ford Coppola)
   4. Vine Hill Wines, Inc. (the Smothers Brothers)
   5. Continental Vineyards (Wayne Rogers)

   a) Santa Cruz
   b) Rutherford (Napa Valley)
   c) Yountville (Napa Valley)
   d) San Luis Obispo
   e) Cloverdale (Sonoma Valley)

6. In *Casablanca,* the classic film about wartime intrigue starring Humphrey Bogart and Ingrid Bergman, Claude Rains plays the role of Chief of Police. When the Germans pay Rick's Café a visit, the Chief of Police stops by their table and recommends a Champagne. What Champagne did he recommend in this famous scene?

ANSWERS

1. *Spring Mountain Vineyards provides the exterior setting for the "Falcon Crest" series. Wine bottled under the Falcon Crest label is also produced at Spring Mountain, as a secondary line to the Spring Mountain label.*

2. *Château Chevalier, modeled after a French château in Arbois, lent its beauty to "The Vintage Years." Let's all hope that the film will be released sometime in the future.*

3. *Claude Rains played the role of a Nazi agent who had hidden a booty of uranium in the wine cellar. As the camera pans across the bottles, it focuses on the 1934 Pommard, inside which his loot is hidden. Hope he enjoyed the wine; it was a superb vintage!*

4. *a)* Killer Bees *was filmed at Captain Neibaum's (Inglenook) mansion, which was built in 1879.*

b) Robert Lawrence Balzer, eminent wine writer, publisher, educator, and author of several books—including the masterpiece Wines of California*—played the role.*

c) In 1976, the great mansion became the property of Francis Ford Coppola, director of The Godfather *and* Apocalypse Now. *The property is now called the Niebaum-Coppola Estate.*

5. *1–c, 2–e, 3–b, 4–a, 5–d.*

6. *"Veuve-Clicquot '26, a good French wine."*

I Am A Vineyard

Following are several descriptions of famous vineyards situated all over the world. Try to identify their names by the clues given.

I am a vineyard . . .

1. . . . with 250 acres planted to Sémillon and Sauvignon Blanc. I am the only property in Sauternes to be classified as a *Grand Cru Premier* (first great growth) in the Classification of 1855. Who am I?

2. . . . with twenty-eight acres in Pomerol. Ninety-five percent of my cultivated land is planted with Merlot. I am named for the apostle Saint Peter, whose likeness appears on my label. Who am I?

3. . . . with 150 acres in Saint-Estèphe. I am classified as a second growth. My vines are cultivated on a slight rise that slopes toward the river Gironde, and I take my name from that hill, which was carpeted in pink heather during the eighteenth century. Who am I?

4. . . . with two hundred acres in Saint-Julien. I am classified as a fourth growth. I am named for the marshal of the English army who fell at the Battle of Castillon in 1453. His title, "Gouverneur de Guienne 1400–1453" is carried on my label, even though no such post ever existed. Who am I?

5. . . . in fact, the biggest vineyard in the Médoc, with nearly four hundred acres at Saint-Laurent. I am classified as a Cru Bourgeois. Who am I?

6. . . . with 17.3 acres in the Côte de Nuits. I am the only estate in Burgundy that has not been divided since I was planted by monks in 1185. I was acquired by the firm of Mommessin in the 1930s. Who am I?

7. . . . with 350 acres in Brouilly. I am the largest Cru estate in Beaujolais. My palace was built by the same craftsmen who erected Versailles, and it is classified as a French historical monument. Who am I?

8. . . . classified as a 100 percent Cru in the Côte de Blancs of the Champagne region. Some of my Chardonnay grapes are used to make a well-known crémant that is produced by Mumm. The name of this lightly sparkling wine is easily confused with my own. Who am I, and what is the name of the wine?

9. . . . with fifty acres planted to very old Zinfandel vines in Sonoma, California. My grapes used to be sold to Ridge Vineyards, who put my name on their label. However, my ownership changed hands in 1971. Since the completion of a new winery in 1977, which bears my name, my entire yield is vinified for our own label. Who am I?

10. . . . in the Carneros district of Napa, California. I am owned by the well-known art collector, René di Rosa, who has adorned my acreage and lake with modern sculptures. I am planted with several grape varieties, which are sold to various wineries. Who am I?

11. . . . with approximately one thousand acres located seventy-five miles south of Peking in Northern China. I have teamed up with Rémy Martin of France, under the name of the Sino-French Joint Venture Winery, Ltd., to produce a semi-dry white wine called Dynasty. Who am I?

12. . . . planted entirely to Cabernet Sauvignon in Tuscany. More specifically, my plot is located in Bolgheri at the Tenuta San Guido, which is owned by the Marchese Mario Incisa della Rocchetta. My wine, which carries my name, is not a DOC. Identifying me is not nearly as difficult as finding my spectacular Cabernet. Very limited supplies are distributed by Antonori. Who am I?

13. . . . with 79.3 acres near Hattenheim in the Rheingau. My most distinctive feature is my surrounding high wall, which was built in the twelfth century by Cistercian monks from the medieval monastery Kloster Eberbach. I am owned by the German state. Who am I?

ANSWERS

1. *Château d'Yquem.*
2. *Château Pétrus.*
3. *Château Montrose.*
4. *Château Talbot.*
5. *Château Larose-Trintaudon.*
6. *Clos-de-Tart.*
7. *Château de la Chaize.*
8. *Cramant is my name; Crémant de Cramant is the name* of the *wine.*
9. *Lytton Springs.*
10. *Winery Lake Vineyard.*
11. *The Vine Farm of Tianjin.*
12. *Sassicaia.*
13. *Steinberg.*